LIFE-CHANGING STORIES

FOR YOUNG WOMEN

ABOUT GROWING WISE

AND GROWING STRONG

A FIRESIDE BOOK
Published by Simon & Schuster
New York London Toronto Sydney Singapore

CHOCOLATE

for a

TEEN'S

SOUL

KAY ALLENBAUGH

FIRESIDE
Rockefeller Center
1230 Avenue of the Americas
New York, NY 10020

FIRESIDE and colophon are registered trademarks
of Simon & Schuster, Inc.
Designed by Bonni Leon

Manufactured in the United States of America

1   3   5   7   9   10   8   6   4   2

Library of Congress Cataloging-in-Publication Data

Chocolate for a teen's soul : life-changing stories for
young women about growing wise and growing strong /
[compiled by] Kay Allenbaugh.
        p.   cm.
1. Young women—Religious life.   I. Allenbaugh, Kay.
            BL625.7 .C48 2000
291.4'32'08352—dc21   00-029366

ISBN 0-684-87081-9

With love and appreciation

to my big sister, Carol,

as we continue to share our journey of

growing wise and growing strong

CONTENTS

III

GROWING PAINS

IV
VISION KEEPERS

V
OVER, UNDER, OR THROUGH

VI
KEEPING THE HIGH WATCH

VII
MAKING MEMORIES

CHOCOLATE

for a

TEEN'S

SOUL

Contents

INTRODUCTION

Rich stories, like chocolate, not only make you feel good, they can also serve as comfort through confusing times. Many of the stories in *Chocolate for a Teen's Soul* are written by young women themselves. You will be amazed at the ability of these writers to tell it like it is about everything from personal triumphs, conflicts, and challenges to most embarrassing moments. Some have had to "draw a line in the sand" as they discovered their own boundaries, while others tell of first loves that were never meant to last. These true stories will help you not only survive, but flourish, as you discover what these young women from the teen years to early twenties have learned—often the hard way—about what it means to be growing wise and growing strong.

As I began this latest volume of *Chocolate* stories, I must admit that at first I felt intimidated, because while I'm young in spirit, my chronological years are showing up in many ways! My desire was to find your collective heartbeat and gather stories that talk about the things that matter most to you. I'm pleased to say that the assortment of stories offered in *Chocolate for a Teen's Soul* are as varied—ranging from poignant to playful—yet connected as each of you are to one another, no matter how old you may be.

Every young woman needs a mentor—someone older whom they can think of as having it all together. Many powerful stories in this book are written for young women by young women themselves, and they are also written by women who will serve as mentors as they look back on their own unforgettable moments with an "if I'd known then what I know now" kind of spirit.

Today, more than ever before, you have the opportunity to be high-tech and wildly creative, and to reinvent your world as you go—but now and then you may find yourself longing for things to be more simple. With so many forces at play, it's no surprise that you may feel grateful for all the opportunities available to you and overwhelmed at the same time. In no other time in your life will you have the youthfulness to climb mountains, the fresh eyes to see the world anew, the passion for first loves, or more desire to be fiercely independent and unique. And with all these opportunities come challenge.

So grab some chocolate and sit with a friend, your older sister, your mom, your mentor, or by yourself and read the stories that are calling to you. May these stories make you laugh and cry, may they provide humor to something you might be taking too seriously, or may they be your companion as you seek answers to your own hurdles. In *Chocolate for a Teen's Soul,* triumph always reigns—and that's the best kind of inspiration of all!

I
ONWARD AND UPWARD

Maturity isn't a product of growing older;
it's a product of growing wiser.

Ann Landers

MAKING IT COUNT

My young eyes grew misty and my inexperienced hands tightly clasped the wooden railing in front of me. This was the funeral of my great-grandfather, an event that had spurred more thought on the subject of death than ever in all of my seven years.

That night, as my father tucked the covers tightly under my chin, I voiced my concerns about dying.

"There's nothing we can do to prevent our fate," my father replied knowingly to my unanswerable questions. "All we can do is make each moment count while we are alive."

Make each moment count. Like a guardian angel, these words have guided me from that day on. They have calmed me when I am nervous. They have given me strength and courage when I am weak. They have made sense to me, like a peanut butter and jelly sandwich makes sense to a hungry child.

Now, five years later, I stand in a cluster of gossiping girls at our middle school dance. The current subject is the adorable new exchange student from Australia, named Jason. The sixth-grade girls have been giggling over his suave accent since his arrival here last Monday.

Suddenly the booming beat of the fast song stops and a slower rhythm fills the bustling gym. There is a scurry of movement as everyone either hurries to find someone to dance with, or admits defeat and heads toward the bleachers to sit down.

"Someone has to ask Jason to dance," one of my friends chirps. Our gazes once again shift to the other side of the gym, where Jason is standing with a group of his friends. All of the girls surrounding me decide that they would rather sit on the bleachers the rest of the night than risk rejection. I, however, decide to face the challenge.

"I'll ask him," I reply courageously, and I turn to walk across the gym, only momentarily glancing back to see the stunned looks on the faces of my friends. The walk across the gym seems endless. I can feel my friends' gazes burning my back. I straighten my collar. My palms are growing moist, and I almost trip over my own feet.

Suddenly I am there. I tap Jason lightly on the shoulder and pray he knows my name. He turns to face me and his sky blue eyes look slightly annoyed. We stand there for a moment while I wait for some acknowledgment that he knows who I am. When I receive none, I say timidly, "Hi, uh, my name's Beth, I'm, um, in your science class."

There is a deathly pause and then finally he replies, "Oh yeah, sixth period, right?"

"Yeah," my voice squeaks and I hurriedly clear my throat. "Um, anyway, would you like to dance with me?"

Silence. His eyes widen slightly and I can see his brain searching to find an excuse. Finally he answers, "Actually, uh, I was kinda planning on sitting this one out."

The words are shattering. Calmly I reply, as if unaffected by this answer, "That's all right." I turn away before he can utter an apology and walk briskly back to the bleachers to join my friends.

Success is mine. It is a different kind of success from what I had hoped for, but I can live with that. The reason I was so quick to decide to ask Jason to dance in the first place is that I realized I had nothing to lose. The only risk I was taking was that of rejection. Taking this risk was more appealing than wasting the whole dance wondering what would have happened. I made those moments count.

Throughout my life there will be victories and defeats. There will not, however, be regrets, because I will know that I have made each moment count. Sometimes it takes a defeat to create a victory.

For the next few minutes, I sit on the bleachers with my friends, explaining the details of my embarrassing story. Finally, the Boyz 2 Men "Down on Bended Knee" song stops. Just as I am about to stand up to join my friends who are already doing the electric slide on the dance floor, I recognize the face of the cute boy in my English class a few feet in front of me. With gleeful astonishment, I realize he is coming my way.

"Hey, Beth, um, I was wondering if you would like to dance with me during the next slow song?" he asks sheepishly.

My hands are shaking slightly. "Yeah, that would be great," I reply with a winning smile. The night is *definitely* still young.

BETH WILLIAMS

COMING OF AGE

*T*he *surprising shine of a small, round ring* winked at me in the mirror. It wasn't so much the silvery glimmer that caught my eye but the ring's unusual location: the belly button of my seventeen-year-old daughter.

We were bustling about in her bathroom, my fingers readying her hair for the high school prom. My baby, who had been unusually small for her age—and whom I straddled on my hip only six years earlier—now towered over me by two inches in height and two sizes in bra cup.

I had braced myself to expect her rebellious streak to occur in unfathomable ways. Strong-willed, introspective, and fiercely independent, my youngest had cloned and assumed my personality. Therefore, despite our differences and the twenty-some year unbridgeable generation gap, I believed that I had snaked a direct line to her soul. A one-way connection, for sure, for she was still unprepared to take my calls or to transmit her messages back to me.

Absorbed in her teenage world with its own quirky blend of music, pathos, rituals, language, and angst, my child was struggling for independence when no such struggle was necessary. Her quest for self-definition occasionally alternated with her insatiable hunger for my attention, or the safety of our home. Yet she bolted out from under my hovering wings the minute that craved nurturing was satisfied.

I can pinpoint the moment my child made her leap into the

world of adulthood. For me, it was the day she told me, matter-of-factly, that she had met a friend in town "for a cup of coffee."

"What did you order?" the dimwitted me asked.

"Duh, Mom. I've just told you. Coffee."

Since when had she stopped drinking hot tea, with two thirds of the cup filled with warm milk, and start to drink—and socialize over—grown-up drinks?

I knew that unless I met these rites of passage with the stoic calm of an undertaker and avoided any retrospection, I'd be accused of being smothering, closed-minded, and—God forbid—old-fashioned. As natural as the role of mother is to me, I'm not to indulge in it. Not even when the voice inside screams for the not-yet-forgotten comfort of two small, warm arms encircling my neck, nor when my ears still hear the whisper wafting through a mist of sweet baby milk-and-powder scent, "Mommy, I love you."

As she pulled her dress over her head, my daughter's camisole raised and exposed the silver ring, naive-looking but for its location. Oblivious to my discovery, my child continued to chat excitedly, while I, a curling iron in my hand, wanted to poke its burning tip right through that grotesque disfigurement of her navel. Was that the same navel against which I used to purr gargling sounds, generating little screams of joy, accompanied by flapping chubby legs and arms?

Well, I negotiated with the powers above. If that's the worst, I'll accept it with bowed head. But could someone please guarantee me that there would be no more? That her prom, her summer job, and her going away to a Midwestern college will satisfy her thirst for self-assertion or whatever else this ring was supposed to signify?

The only thing I could do to minimize the risk of more such idiosyncrasies was to keep mum, or else I'd surely take the wind of freedom out of my daughter's sails. If she failed to gain the sense of specialness out of her belly button embellishment, she'd seek a new one. And if I invaded that next one, there might be more.

Two nights later, exhausted from a long weekend of prom partying, the ritual of staying out all night played out, she allowed me the now rare delight of tucking her into bed. From her freckled face, framed by the pillow, those open, trusting eyes I so love looked on me.

She wasn't going to say it, so I volunteered. "Can I sing you a lullaby?" I asked. And she, with the same satisfied smile that had scrunched her round cheeks into an irresistible beam at age four, nestled her head in my lap. "Okay," she said. She curled up and closed her eyes, ready to be my child again.

TALIA CARNER

I will write myself into well-being.
NANCY MAIRS

DIVING FOR IT

*I*didn't have such an easy time of it in high school. It seemed as though something always happened to throw me off-center. But when I sat down in English Composition class that day, I thought my luck had changed. I could not have imagined the surprise that awaited no matter how hard I tried.

At first I thought it was a good thing. A terrific thing. My first poem, and beside it, in big red letters, not only an A but an A+. A smile formed, the kind of smile that comes upon you from some unbidden place when you do something for the first time—and someone likes it.

With a sense of excitement, I read the words beside it, also in red. *Excellent, but I don't think you wrote it,* the words said.

Simple as that. *But I don't think you wrote it.* The words seemed unfathomable to me. Stunned, I watched as before my eyes my perfect day blew up as if it had been hit by mortar fire. Without thinking about it, I coughed, trying in vain to avoid the flying metal that pierced my innocence. How could she think . . . What in the world? . . . Me? My poem—a fake?

My pride of accomplishment felt buffeted. My shoulders slumped. Well, maybe this was a normal day. I'd been thrown

off-center again. But no, this felt much bigger. Much more personal. And the instigator of my demise was, of all people, my
teacher. Shirley. I remember her first name now, but not her last.
That would be giving her too much notice.

In my mind, I played over various scenarios. If only she had
asked me if I'd written it. If only—and I sadly knew she hadn't felt
this—if only she had *hoped* I had written it. And then she would
have asked me *how* I wrote it. How did this philosophical poem
about the cottonballs falling from a cottonwood tree come
from—ah . . . someone like you? Now I knew more than I
wanted to know. In writing class, I had looked into the soul of
Shirley, and found out all too clearly the limits of her thinking.

I looked at her often that day. I sat there, looking into a new
force in my life. Expecting her to fix it. To come over to my desk
and talk it over. But this woman was serious. Before I left class, I
decided one thing. I was mad.

At home that afternoon, I went for a walk. A long walk. Fortunately, I called the great forests outside of town my home.
Tucked away between two mountain rivers, our home offered
access to a kind of peace that seeped into you without a person
needing to ask. So I took the feeling of the red-inked slight with
me, out into the place where ancient boughs of fir trees swept
around me, with a healing quality.

Each step seemed to stir something good, matching my anger
and sorrow with a counterbalance. Clear, sweet air met the ten-
sion in my lungs. And soon I watched the river's life. First the
sparrows flying effortlessly over the river's surface. Watch,
watch, the river seemed to say. Then I saw it—small birds called
water dippers, hopping from river rock to river rock, balancing
perfectly on the stones and then diving right in. And then out, as
if nothing had happened. Nothing they couldn't handle, anyway!
I expelled the air in my lungs, letting go of the day's stress with it
as I laughed along with the daring water dippers.

That evening, I returned to my home, and wrote. I wrote

twenty new poems that night, twenty poems I didn't know I had
in me.

And the next day, feeling a bit like an "in-charge" water dipper,
facing the river with audacity, I plunked my sheaf of white
pages, peppered with poems, crisply on her desk. In front of her.
In front of Shirley.

I didn't ask her anything. I'd learned something from that colorful river bird. I simply said, "You didn't think I wrote that
poem." She looked at me, like a blue jay that's wanting to steal
all the bread, but wary that you'll chase him off. "So I wrote
some more."

I decided that my audacity was stronger than her peskiness. So
I stood there a moment, but she never answered. Reclaiming my
sense of accomplishment, I took my seat again, but I didn't really
occupy that chair anymore. She hadn't earned my writer's trust.
After class, I approached my other English teacher, the inspiring
but very truthful Mrs. Parmenter, whose desk always held a vase
of flowers on it. After I told her what happened, her eyes crin-
kled, and I felt her reach out to me without using her hands. It
was more like a cloud of hope that comforted me. That renewed
my faith. And that lent its power to fight those who would harm
someone's budding creativity.

I asked Mrs. Parmenter how she arranged the beautiful flowers upon her desk.

"I just put them in, and they seem to fall naturally into place."

That was the kind of woman who believed in something.
Sharing copies of all my poems with Mrs. Parmenter, I received
not only her honest approval, but her respect as well. As if giving
me her own bouquet of flowers, her voice formed words I'll
never forget. "These should be published," she said.

And she did one more thing. She put her hand on my shoulder, and smiled right into my heart.

I learned strength that day. Like those river birds, I just dived
right in, and in exchange I grew stronger and more centered. I

went on to get an A+ for the term from Shirley. But I felt most grateful to a firm but gentle Mrs. Parmenter, and the colorful antics of a water dipper!

I had no idea—well, yes I did. I somehow knew that poetry was *mine*. My gift. When you feel a big response, you know it must be your gift. But I didn't know I would become a writing teacher—and an award-winning poet. I never knew that people who didn't think they could write a poem would just start writing them in my classes. But I somehow did know that when I gave them an assignment *to write about someone who has affected your life*, I would say, "Sometimes that person is a blessing from the start, and sometimes, like the teacher who challenged my authorship, the person is a blessing—in disguise. Don't miss out on the gifts that come from facing the people who challenge you, even in an unkind way. Each time you stand up, you change your life."

I think now that if Shirley had not challenged my poetry skills, not to mention my pride and self-respect, I might not have gone home and written those twenty new poems. And I might not have developed a little uppity toughness that goes with any desire to do something good. But today, most of all, with each poem and each accomplishment, I think of Mrs. Parmenter. And I know she must be happy that it's harder to throw me off balance now. Holding on to your pride may be hard in high school, but sometimes you have to fight for it—even dive for it. And honor the gifts of who you are.

SHEILA STEPHENS

My heart is happy, my mind is free
I had a father who talked with me.
HILDA BIGELOW

BIG HILLS

"**W**ow," Dad said, wiping the sweat off his brow and tilting his head back. "Will you look at that thing. It's huge! Wanna go?"

I was fourteen years old, and we were on a family vacation at Cedar Point amusement park in Sandusky, Ohio. My father's invitation to ride the Mean Streak roller coaster, the rocket ship of my teenage dreams, hung in the air like a poster in my room. He and I were alike. We had the same desire for thrill seeking running in our veins.

"What will it be like?" I asked my mom.

She rolled her eyes and shrugged. "I don't know, and I have no desire to ride those things."

"Why?"

"I just don't like big hills."

Dad and I waited in the long line, the air hot and the pavement hotter. I had lots of time to watch the roller coaster go up and down the hills, and see what the people inside the cars looked like.

Just like Dad, I had to tilt my head over really far to see the top of the ride. I heard the whisklike rumble above and around us.

And I could hear the people screaming their lungs out, but it didn't sound as if it came from a free-spirited thrill. I couldn't help but wonder at how safe it was.

"Dad, do you hear all those people screaming because they are scared?"

"Oh, lots of people scream on roller coasters because it's thrilling. Don't worry, you'll like it," he said, offering me all the assurance he thought I needed.

My teenage pride kicked in. "I'm not worried. I was just asking you a question," I said with irritation.

"Are you scared?" Dad had a way of hitting the mark.

"No, it's just a ride. It'll be over before I know it . . . right?" That's what he'd told me earlier, before I was staring up at this wooden mountain of a thing.

"That's right, it's going to be fun, and you get to tell your sister and mom what chickens they are," he said, and we both laughed. Not only was I stepping into a new world, but I had my dad at my side. I thought of Mom and my younger sister Sara sitting at one of the picnic tables a ways off. How boring for them. They were probably so bored that they were having second thoughts. Dad and I were the only ones who knew how to have fun in this family!

Two older girls chattered in front of us. They kept saying they should turn around now, before it was too late. Noticing how I was listening to them, Dad turned to me and graciously gave me a way out. "Well, what do you think? Maybe we should take their advice and bail out right now."

Somehow the release within his words helped me settle down the churning in my body. "Dad! You aren't serious, are you? I thought you said coasters were nothing once you got on one?"

"No, calm down. I'm just joking. They're nothing after you've been on one." I though he was reassuring me, but could he have been reassuring himself? I studied his face just as I had studied the faces of the older girls in front of me. It looked kind of uptight, but that was probably because it was so hot. With his arms crossed, he stood there watching the next coaster whiz by us. I started to feel shaky and nervous all over again.

"Well, only about fifteen minutes and it will be time for our death ride!"

"Dad!" I glared at him, then softened. "Are you scared?"

"Well, to tell you the truth, girl, I have never been on one quite this big." He laughed, a little quieter this time.

As we made our way inside the building, I felt Dad and me becoming closer, even though he was of no help. He kept teasing, now, that the roller coaster would get stuck.

"Does that really happen?" I asked, half doubting him, half believing him.

"Yeah, sometimes they have to send helicopters up to get you out." He looked amused. I wondered. I'd heard about people getting sick and it landing on other people's heads. I thought that was the worst! Getting stuck I could not take. I started to panic.

Now we could see people getting off the cars—their faces flushed, their eyes bugging out. I studied each face, hoping to find some inner strength from them. Most wore a smile or had at least a hint of it, which made me feel a little less worried. My life was in their hands. I felt each face made a promise to me. All of a sudden, a girl who looked exactly like me and about my age let out a pitiful moan as she practically ran through the exit gate, holding her stomach with both hands.

"Dad . . ."

"I know what you see, but don't worry. Trust me, you'll like it." But there was no more time to be worried now. It was our turn. I had moved beyond the boring picnic tables and into another world. As I climbed into the ride, I noticed that we were seated in the first car. I tried to pull the bar down. "It won't go down! It's not locking! Dad!— Oh, there."

"Here we go, girl!" I looked at Dad. He was smiling but holding on tight. I tried to do the same. The coaster suddenly lurched forward, and we began climbing the big hill with the biggest drop. I could feel the saliva in my mouth working.

"Oh my gosh, Dad. Look down!"

"No, thanks, I'll pass and look at the floor!"

"Dad, put your arm around me. I hate this feeling! Dad?"

"Okay! Here we go!" he yelled. We had made it to the top. For a tiny second the roller coaster stopped—a tiny second that felt like a lifetime. I told myself to keep swallowing.

"I want to get off!" I screamed, my logic lost in the rumble of the air.

As we dropped from this "hill" that was certainly a mountain, I could feel my skin plastered to my bones. No breath could escape my mouth. And then . . . it was so fast that it ended before I knew it. The big one, anyway. Then we cruised around little hills and curves, and I decided, this isn't so bad. As a smile began to appear on my own face, I saw Dad laughing and screaming at the same time, but I was too shocked to pry my lips any wider. I noticed he no longer had his protective arm around me, but held on tight to the bar with both hands, just like me. My own terror had turned my knuckles white as they held the safety bar so tightly, it was hard to move them off.

As we coasted to a stop, I felt proud. *I've done it,* I thought, and walked off with a certain coolness, shoulders back, head held high. *It wasn't so bad,* I told myself, as Dad talked nonstop in my ear.

"Well, that was great! What did you think of that hill? I was scared out of my mind!"

"You were?" I asked.

"Yes! You know when you asked me to put my arm around you? I could only do it for about two seconds 'cause I needed to hold on," he admitted, laughing at himself.

"You were scared too?"

"Of course! That's half the fun!" He looked at me. "I'm proud of us," he said, as he put his arm back around me. I heard the "proud," and I also heard the "us." My dad and I, not content to sit around the picnic tables. My dad and I, partners, both adventurous and both scared. Maybe if he was scared, it meant I could do something like this again—on my own, I thought. But I knew, as I flashed ahead, looking at the breadth of my life, that whatever hill—or mountain—I climbed in the future, I wouldn't be alone. My dad would somehow be at my side. Maybe even white-knuckled, but laughing, saying into my ear, "Wasn't that great, the way you dealt with that fear? And what did you think of that hill?"

REBECCA L. ALLOR

THE "IN" CROWD

*A*ll I ever wanted was to be popular. Have the coolest friends. Be in a hot rock band and date the best-looking men—simple wishes for a young girl like me. Some of my dreams even came true. I started a rock band. And the cutest guy at Melbourne High School in Florida even asked me out.

I said yes, of course, but within a week, he complained, "Your hips are too big. You need to lose weight to look thin like the other girls in your band and on the beach."

Immediately, I tried several diets. On one, I ate grapefruit and vegetables only—and I felt faint and had to eat "real food." The second week I tried skipping breakfast and dinner. When I did that, I became so hungry by the time dinner came, I splurged and eventually started gaining weight. I added ten pounds in a month trying to please my new boyfriend. Instead of praising my efforts, he cut me down even more. "You look like a whale," he said, making me feel not as pretty as my other friends who wanted to date him. I felt self-conscious and didn't want to lose him as a boyfriend, so I desperately searched for a way to lose the pounds that were keeping him at bay. I was 110 pounds, a complete blimp!

Other girls in my school were doing the same thing in the bathroom to lose weight, and they never suffered any permanent damage. I wouldn't either. All I ever wanted was to be as pretty as a model. I wanted my boyfriend to look at me the same way he looked at those bikini poster girls.

Once a day turned into three forced vomits. Malnourished, I was constantly hungry, so I ate more—and threw up more. It wasn't until I started gaining water weight and tried to quit that I realized I couldn't stop the cycle. As soon as I got up from the table, my stomach began convulsing. My own stomach somehow believed that was what it was supposed to do now. I would constantly have to run from the table. I was throwing up without even sticking my finger down my throat or even wanting to! I wasn't in control anymore—of my weight or my life.

No one ever mentioned to me that if you force yourself to vomit after you eat, you actually retain water, lose hair, ruin the enamel on your teeth, get serious stomach ailments, and worse—have no power to halt the process!

I needed help. My boyfriend and my weight were the least of my problems now, and I knew it. At age fifteen I didn't know what to do. Desperate for a solution, I broke down into tears and confided in the only person I could trust.

"Mom, I'm sick. I tried forcing myself to throw up to lose weight, now I am vomiting every day. I can't stop, and I'm afraid I'm going to die."

I locked myself in my room the entire night. The next morning my mom woke me up to tell me I had a doctor's appointment. After the initial meeting, I was placed in a hospital. My blood work indicated that I was dehydrated and starving. They wouldn't release me for months. I felt all alone. I missed a year of school. I had to be tutored to make up the work so I wouldn't be held back. It took several types of medicines and months of counseling before my bulimia was under control.

My boyfriend left me. He dumped me because dates in the hospital weren't much fun. Most of my friends didn't understand and stopped coming to see me. Even a family member made jokes that I must be making this all up for attention. I can't tell you how much that hurt.

But, I'm finally okay. I'm at peace.

It took one year of medication and counseling to realize that if people didn't appreciate me for who I am no matter what weight I am, then they're not worth knowing in the first place.

I learned that the hard way, a lesson I'll never forget. Being popular is an artificial notion. Once I knew I was "enough," it didn't matter what other people thought. If you love and believe in yourself, you are in the "in" crowd.

MICHELE WALLACE CAMPANELLI

MISS CONGENIALITY
AND MORE

"**M**om, you know the only thing I'm really hoping will not happen?" my niece Kim told my sister as she brushed her long, auburn hair.

"What is it, honey?" her mother asked.

"I absolutely do *not* want to win the Miss Congeniality title."

At seventeen, Kim had exercised unusual courage and entered a Georgia beauty pageant. She had grown up "different" all her life. Born weighing 2.8 pounds, she was lucky to be alive at all. Cerebral palsy seemed an acceptable price to pay for her presence on earth.

But that price loomed large as Kim endured multiple surgeries before the age of ten. She worked mightily to do the things that came so naturally to other kids, and she absorbed the stares and sympathy of strangers as other kids teased her for her "Minnie Mouse" stick-thin legs in braces.

"In my case, Miss Congeniality would be a sympathy vote. I want to win without anybody's pity."

"Are you sure you want to do this at all?" her mother asked. Always encouraging Kim toward independence and full participation, my sister Carol silenced her own qualms about beauty pageants. Carol had many years of practice at flinching at each of Kim's wounds and marveling as her daughter grew in determination and wisdom.

April 1997, the big night. After three rounds of judging, after Kim's triumphantly successful stroll down the runway in her midnight-blue evening gown, the music signaled the announcement of awards.

"Miss Congeniality . . . Kim Stohlmann."

Kim's eyes widened instantly as she squealed with unexpected delight. Her hands flew up to cover her mouth. Maybe it wasn't so bad to be selected for the spotlight after all. The flowers, the applause, the admiring looks from all the contestants who had voted for her warm heart and her spunky spirit, the tears she didn't see in her mother's eyes, yet felt stinging in her own. There was a sudden magic in the moment that surprised her. She was still caught in the thrill as she heard the music rise again for the rest of the show. The microphone crackled an instant, and the announcer spoke in deeper, melodious tones.

"The winner of the title of third runner-up would be called upon to assume the crown if other winners were prevented by circumstances from fulfilling their role. And now, our third runner-up . . . Kim Stohlmann."

She had won.

Vindicated.

Courageous.

Beautiful.

Kim Stohlmann.

MAGGIE BEDROSIAN

TRUE COLORS

*I*t's the last day of school before the December break in the small town of Cadillac, Michigan. The middle and high schools sit side by side across the road from the lake, and I watch kids spilling down the sidewalk, free at last from the classroom confines for a scant two weeks. Their backpacks, slung over narrow shoulders, are stuffed with holiday homework, but there is a gaiety of spirit that is infectious.

I don't "belong" to any children, but I like to watch them as I drive to my job as reporter-observer at the local newspaper. These kids are nothing like we used to be, I think. Just look at those haircuts—either no hair at all, or cuts that look like their mom puts a bowl over their heads and shaves off whatever hangs below the rim. And those baggy, foot-tripping pants—surely those can't be comfortable! Ours were baggy, yes, but only from the knee down. Elephant bells—now, those were cool. Our hip huggers stayed nicely in place. Theirs look dangerous.

Across from the education complex, terns and gulls and unlimited ducks ruffle their feathers against the frigid temperatures, squawking among themselves on the shore of Lake Cadillac. A teenager meets them in the parking lot, tugging from his pocket a well-worn, white-bread sandwich, ignored at lunchtime. He gives the birds the lot. It's a very tender scene, I think as I drive on. He might just as well have tossed it in the trash bin, but he didn't. I wonder why?

Kids everywhere. I like to see how these individuals walk, carrying their fledgling pride, and I like puzzling out what they want to be when they "grow up." Environmentalists, I'll bet. Foresters. Marine scientists. Will they make it, or will they give up when they learn about "real life"? Our generation was going to change the world, and certainly we did—not always for the better. We yelled, "Give peace a chance," and let the ozone be destroyed. We screamed, "Make love, not war," and jumped from relationship to relationship as our country got involved in conflict after conflict. We even advocated, "Power to the people," and then amassed status cars and turned a blind eye to the air pollution they caused.

We set excellent bad examples.

Although these children are just children, they paid close attention to us. When I was a teenager, my dream was to be the exact opposite of what the older generation represented. Not for me the slings and arrows of suburban discontent—oh no. My age group didn't invent discontent, but we sure put a name to it. Kent State. Woodstock. The Black Panthers. Countless sit-ins, Man, we were radical!

In my own way, I still am; hence, the career as a reporter. I write about the environment, drive a truck, still wear blue jeans and let my hair hang long, well into my forties. The ideals of the peace movement that came out of the 1960s and '70s evolved into my twenty-five-year Buddhist practice. And I'm still trying to give peace a chance on a daily basis.

The quintessential symbol of my younger years—what summed it up for me—was the peace sign. I remember Richard Milhouse Nixon abusing that two-fingered salute—*our* symbol of peace—even as he ordered the bombs that rained upon Vietnam. We hated him for it.

But all that aside, the peace sign, the extended "V" of index and middle fingers, symbolized what a frustrated generation was trying to teach its elders: Let's do things differently. Let's take care of each other and our planet. Let's stop the senselessness of war.

In came disco, the Material Girl, American Express cards, the

Internet, paisley power ties, and fleeting status. What happened to those sweet, pure peaceniks we once thought we were? Where did all the flowers go?

I mourn this passing as I drive by the schoolkids. I feel sad they never saw us the way we saw ourselves back then. They never saw our desire to, above all else, change the world. And now it's too late; all they see are adults flying past in sport utility vehicles on the way to the mall.

Of what do these children dream? How will their idealism manifest? I used to think we must have disappointed them.

But now I know better.

Because on this day I follow a big yellow school bus up to a red traffic light, just beyond the school. The back half of the bus is filled with young faces staring out at me. I sing out "True Colors" along with Phil Collins on my CD player. Groovin' out, man.

Then, one face in particular leaps out at me from the rear window of the bus: Two solemn little-girl eyes hold all the accusatory wisdom of the ages in her otherwise-expressionless face. She stares me down hard—checks me out thoroughly—and then, in a moment of enlightenment, she decides to trust me.

It is a moment of grace, that smile from those sweet lips in the back of the bus. She catches me by surprise, but I soldier on, smile back, singing, "True colors are shining through . . . I see your true colors, and that's why I love you. . . ."

She saw my true colors, despite my adulthood.

And then, slowly, she raises a tiny arm. It pauses, her fist just north of her right shoulder, and her fingers part into the sacred, time-honored "V" of peace.

My gosh. She is speaking my lingo.

What else could I do? Tears fill my eyes, and I raise my own hand and "V" her right back. We grin at each other through our separate windows.

Then, one by one, the other kids on the back of the bus raise their own Vs. Our hearts connect, and suddenly there are no differences, no generations between us. I sing on, "So don't be afraid to let them show, your true colors, true colors, are beautiful" while watching a bus full of children, lead by a special girl, waving for peace.

JENNIFER GORDON GRAY

With the gift of listening comes the gift of healing.
CATHERINE DE HUECK DOHERTY

SECOND ACT

I was a fatso kid, a chunky adolescent, and an over-weight teenager. I ate for comfort through an unhappy childhood, and then out of habit. I buried my negative thoughts about myself beneath macaroni and cheese, raw hot dogs, and potato chips. My senior year in college, when I finally pulled myself up from underneath all the grease and fast food long enough to listen to what that little intuitive voice inside my brain had to say to me, I cringed, thinking I would hear terrible, scarring words. Instead, I was gentle with myself. I let myself cry and rock with my arms held tight around my body, hugging my three raggedy childhood blankies to my chest.

Then I got to work. Over the course of three years, I exercised and started eating healthier than I ever had in my entire life. I began to lose the weight. The planes of my face materialized and I saw the shape of my chin, the line of my cheekbones, the slope of my jaw. I saw me.

During the dip after graduate school and before my first real job in the professional world, I'd been exploring my deepest dreams and desires. I kept thinking that my wanting to be an actress started when I was a little girl. I'd always dismissed my desire to act because I thought it was vain of me to want to be on stage. And my body image was so horrible that the very thought of getting up in front of an audience and being entirely at their mercy scared me a lot.

One gray January day in 1998, I was jogging and got a stitch in my side. I slowed to a walk, breathing shallowly and watching the cars whistle along the pavement beside me through the fog. I started to pray as I walked, saying "Okay, God, I haven't prayed since I was a little girl, but if you're going to speak through me, I'll listen. Am I supposed to act? Aren't I being vain to want to?" At that exact moment, as soon as I had finished the thought, the stitch in my side intensified, and I gasped out loud, nearly doubling over. Tears came to my eyes and I started hyperventilating because it hurt so bad. In the two years I'd been running, I'd never experienced a cramp like this.

As suddenly as the cramp came, I realized my prayer for guidance had been answered. I was being given a message: I was *not* being vain. I could experience the fruits of my labor over the last three years but only if I stopped thinking negatively about myself.

Just as suddenly I had an image. I was on the cover of *Vanity Fair* magazine with makeup, hair, French manicure, dressed all in black. My hands were splayed across my stomach, pulling my shirt up and my pants down a little so the vivid white stretch mark scars, slicing bars across my belly, were on display for the world to see. The tracks of my struggle, the footprints of my journey.

I strode along, my breath freezing in the air, and started crying. The little girl still living inside my heart kept repeating, *Okay, but I'm scared! They're going to make fun of me!* And I sobbed down the street, stumbling over spills of icy snow.

It's now been over a year that I set my fears aside and boldly stepped onto the stage. Since then, I've attended acting classes and been in two local plays, and I no longer entertain negative thoughts about myself. Taking all the time I need, I'm perfecting

THE HAND-ME-DOWN

I *was eleven when my grandparents and I fled our* Soviet-occupied country, Hungary, into neighboring Austria, with our only worldly possessions—the clothes on our backs. Soon we were transported to a displaced-persons camp, where we joined other refugees. The year was 1947.

Our new home, D.P. Camp Spittal, was a self-contained world of barracks lined up like soldiers as far as the eye could see. Although the camp was cramped and dismal, it was an improvement over the life we had known in our war-torn country over the past six years. We had a roof over our heads, we were fed daily, and we were clothed from the donations of clothing that arrived regularly from the United States and other countries.

Since most of us in the camp had no money to speak of, we especially looked forward to the distribution of clothes, which usually took place in the spring and in the fall. And if the clothes came from America, we fingered them in awe, for that's where most of us hoped to immigrate.

Of course, the clothes weren't new, but they were clean and good and we were grateful to get them. This also meant that no one outshone anyone else in the camp. We were equal in our hand-me-downs. Until the fall of 1950, that is, when Providence smiled on me and allowed me—a girl used to having nothing nice—to shine for a while.

We were lined up at the distribution center again for our winter garments when the man in charge made an announcement.

"This year a rich lady in America donated something rare to

my craft and putting my body on display. Nobody's made fun of me—they've praised my abilities instead.

Like panning for ore, I found the good stuff inside of me after digging down deep. At first I was unrecognizable, until polished and primed. Now I shine with brilliance, just like 24-karat gold.

JACQUELYN B. FLETCHER

the refugee effort. It is this beautiful multicolored fur coat in a young girl's size." He held up the coat for everyone to see. Oohs and ahhs rang out throughout the crowd.

"Since we only have one coat, and many young girls, we've decided to have a drawing for it. Girls will come up and try it on, and if it fits, they will write their name on a piece of paper and drop it in this box. Then we'll draw the name of the winner."

"That coat looks like it will fit you perfectly," Grandmother said. "Go try it on and put your name in the box." The coat was soft, plush, and beautiful to the touch, and I hankered to own it! So did many other girls. After what seemed like eternity, a small girl was asked to reach into the box and draw a name.

"Renie Szilak," the man shouted, waving a piece of paper in the air. "Come on up, young lady, and get your coat."

I stood there in a daze, not quite believing it was true, until Grandmother nudged me on. I walked up, feeling the hundreds of eyes watching me. And when I walked back, wearing the coat, I heard a voice in the crowd call out, "You look just like a real princess now." It was Tibor's voice, the cutest boy in our school. I blushed, but I hoped that I was walking regally, the way a real princess would!

"I can't believe some girl in America gave up this coat," I told my friend Piri on the way back to our barrack.

"Maybe it no longer fit her," Piri said.

"But it's so beautiful. I won't give it up even after it no longer fits," I vowed. "I'll keep it forever!"

Piri was two years younger than I was and had become the closest thing to a sister I would ever have. We lived in the same barrack, and since her father was ill and needed her mother at his side most of the time, she spent much of her time with my family and me. And since both of our families had applied for immigration to the United States, a lot of that time was taken up with dreaming about our future lives there.

That winter when I'd turned fourteen, I was a refugee-camp

princess! Everywhere I went in my new coat, admiring glances followed, and when I walked to school, boys who usually ambushed the girls with snowballs let me walk by untouched. One day, while Piri and I walked through the town of Spittal, an Austrian girl called out, "Hey, D.P. girl, where did you get that beautiful coat?"

"It came from America," I boasted, tossing my blond locks, enjoying the attention.

Then spring arrived, and I reluctantly put the coat in a box and shoved it under my sleeping cot in the barrack. But I knew it would be there for me next winter.

Not long after, we received the news we had been waiting for. Our papers had been approved, and in September we would board the ship taking us to our new country, the United States of America! I hurried to tell Piri the good news, hoping their papers had come through too. I found her outside, sad-faced, her eyes red from crying.

"What's wrong?" I asked, not wanting to know the answer.

"We haven't been approved. They say Papa has TB. Only healthy people can go to America," she replied quietly, turning my world upside-down.

Of course, we spent the remaining few months glued to each other, but inevitably, the day we had to part arrived.

On August 1, 1951, Piri and I were about to say our last farewell before we boarded the transport truck already filling up with people. The truck was to take us to Salzburg, where our vaccinations would be updated before we would go on to the port of Bremen, Germany, to board the ship taking us to our new country.

"Don't forget me. Write to me," Piri said, hugging me, tears rolling down her pale cheeks. Her mother, standing next to her, was crying too. Suddenly, the realization hit that not only would we never see each other again, but they would not be going on to a new life in a new country, and I had to ease her distress. So I broke away and ran after Grandfather, just boarding the truck with a large box in his hand. I yanked the box from him without an explanation and raced back to Piri's side.

"I want you to have the coat. I love you, little sister, and I'll write as soon as we have a permanent address," I said, shoving the box into her hands.

"But you said you'd never give up the coat . . ." Piri began.

"I'm not giving it up. I'm passing it on to my little sister." Then I ran to climb aboard the truck, which was about to leave without me. But I'll never forget the expression on Piri's face, as she stood there teary-eyed, clutching the box, teetering between sadness and gladness. That was the moment I, a mostly selfish fourteen-year-old, discovered the joy of giving.

It was mid-November by the time I could send an address to Piri. I received her jubilant reply a few days before Christmas 1951. There was a photo with the letter, too. It showed a girl with curly black hair and a beaming smile. She wore a beautiful, multicolored fur coat and she looked just like a real princess in it. And that made my heart glad.

RENIE SZILAK BURGHARDT

II
WHAT IS THIS THING
CALLED LOVE?

When I open my heart, I see things differently.

Jo Anna Burns-Miller

LOVE ON THE YELLOW BRICK ROAD

*O*ne day my best friend, Sarah, had the impulsive idea to introduce me to Kevin, a boy she'd first met in elementary school. "Don't even go there," I said before she clicked-dialed-clicked her phone to hook us both up with some guy I didn't even know.

"Kevin, it's Sarah. I've got my friend Ranae on too."

Great, I thought. *I'm committed.* But Kevin's voice—deep, rich, and sweet, like vanilla ice cream in a slow melt over hot apple pie—changed that. "Ranae, what's goin' on?" I got this big dopey smile on my face before I sank to the floor, closed my eyes, and let his voice soak through me. The three of us were on the phone, but as Kevin and I talked, Sarah ceased to exist even when she was the one talking. Every day for the next two months his voice made me feel special.

The first time we met face-to-face was at the mall. We got there at exactly the same time. She hissed, "There's Kevin, right in front of you!" Staring at the back of his head, my knees turned to Jell-O. A lump the size of Mt. Everest stuck in my throat. He stood with another guy, and as I watched him from the back he turned. Boy, I thought, he looks as nervous as I feel.

I gave my friend a shove in his direction, "Go talk to him for me. Tell him to meet me in Bath and Body Works." She rolled her eyes, shook her head, and went in for the kill while I darted into the store. A few minutes later he stood just inside the door and looked uncomfortable next to a display of watermelon bath gel. I held my breath, strode up to him, and handed him a penny. I blurted out something about good luck. Lame, lame, lame. I wanted to walk away. I wanted to hide.

"Hey, Ranae. What's goin' on?" He spoke as if he had just missed the lameness of my last thirty seconds, and the only thing that kept my knees from buckling was the arm he put around my shoulder. He smelled like a cross between Tommy Hilfiger and God. I could have collapsed or run a marathon, I'm not sure which, but instead, we went for ice cream. When the scooper guy handed me my cup, the spoon bounced up and flipped little Rocky Road chunks on Kevin's face. I stopped breathing, but Kevin just turned red and laughed. I hoped Rocky Road wasn't some kind of weird omen for us.

Two weeks later, the day before my sixteenth birthday, and five days before Valentine's Day, we officially became a couple. We were inseparable and in love and everything about sixteen was sweet, sweet, sweet. Kevin became my first kiss—in fact, he became a lot of firsts in the love department. One night he climbed the balcony to bring me hot soup when I was sick, so naturally, "You and Me" from *Romeo and Juliet* became our song. We hoarded pop-can tops to trade for kisses. One top for one kiss, no cheating. We saved quarters for green gemstones out of the vending machines in the mall where we first met. Green for the Emerald City. Green for his eyes.

Kevin brought out the best in me. I loved everything about him, but what I loved most was everything about us. That's why I surprised myself by breaking up with him. How do I explain this? You know how being with somebody all the time kind of makes you forget who *you* are, even though you really like being together. Whatever, "You and Me" was over.

After I broke up with Kevin, I lost track of time. The days melted into one big glob of Rocky Road. I'd lost myself when we were together, and now that I'd lost him, I felt as if I'd lost the best part of what I'd found in myself with him.

One night, I visited Kevin's best friend, kind of hoping Kevin would show up. He did, and being in the same room was strange, awkward, and painful. Everything we'd once shared sat in an invisible lump on the couch between us while the TV flickered in front of us. We tried hard to resist each other. I felt a little sick. I pulled out my strawberry Chapstick and smoothed it on my aching lips. Lips that ached not only from a day in the sun but for a kiss. Kevin's green eyes met my cornflower blue ones, and he burst into tears while his best friend and girlfriend sat lip-locked in a chair across the room.

Kevin's friend broke his hold and asked, "What's wrong with him?" as Kevin rushed past them on his way out. I shrugged.

Months later I saw Kevin again, and in a moment I was weak-kneed once more. We decided we couldn't be without each other, so we got back together. We drifted along the yellow brick road of love for a while, me headed straight for the Emerald City, ignoring warning signs along the way. The pop-top kisses weren't as electric or often. The green gemstones didn't seem as hopelessly romantic either, but I was in love with the idea of being in love, until clicking my heels three times and making a wish just didn't work anymore. This time, Kevin dumped me and I cried.

The day he left me, I went home and burned everything that reminded me of him. The pop tops and green gemstones, the top I wore the day we met at the mall, I even emptied three cans of chicken noodle soup down the disposal and threw the cans in the fire. I traded all my quarters for dollars and smaller change. I thought that by getting rid of everything "Kevin," I could get rid of all that hurt and the leftover love I didn't want aching away inside me.

Over time I healed and so did Kevin. In a way, we healed together, just as we had loved together. Sometimes, when I'm walking the mall alone and I see a quarter machine with green gemstones, I get one to remind me of my first love. To remember that every love is one more jewel on my way to the Emerald City.

RANAE QUASHNOCK

ROLLER SKATES AND LICENSE PLATES

*S*creech . . . *swish* . . . *screech* . . . *swish* . . . My dad really needs to oil my swing set. The hairs on the back of my neck are on end because I know that Drew is watching me. My stomach doesn't usually feel this queasy when I swing. Maybe I shouldn't go as high. The shadow of Drew's bike reaches the grass in front of me from the top of the hill where he is perched. Why doesn't he just come down and play with me? Well, I'll show him.

I jump off the swing and march directly up the stairs to my back door without even a glance back. I'd rather play in the front yard anyway. How convenient for him that his best friend lives across the street from me. Now he can sit and talk about me while he stares. I feel like one of those pimples that you try to hide; only everyone sees it and relishes in gazing at it as if at any minute it will explode.

Back at school, there's lots of giggling as I walk by his lunch table. Why is he doing this to me? If he doesn't stop, I won't be able to show my face at the skating rink Saturday night. There he would be able to humiliate me to music as the reflections of the disco ball chase me. If I go, then everyone will know my embarrassing secret. Drew Seek, the cutest boy in the fourth grade . . . hates me!

Then later that week: *Knock, knock.* "Hi, Mrs. Carrington. My name is Drew Seek. I was wondering if Michelle could, uh, come swimming at my house? My mom is home, sh-she said you can call her." Oh my gosh! Is it safe for my heart to beat this fast? I didn't know the tops of my arms could sweat like that. My mom broke into my panic, "Michelle? You have a visitor. Do you want to go swimming at Drew's?" Now, this is the same boy who has tortured me for weeks. "Sure."

After that afternoon, I couldn't wait to go roller-skating. I met Drew there on Saturday night, the most popular night to go. Everyone would be there.

Drew and I skated together. Well, we skated next to each other. The lights dimmed as the disc jockey called for couples only to the floor. I can't believe I'm a couple! The song was "When I Need You," by Leo Sayer. Both of us were too shy to hold hands. So we skated next to each other, occasionally, on accident bumping our shoulders together. It's probably best that we didn't hold hands. I wasn't feeling so good, and my hands were clammy. Maybe I was catching a cold.

I soon realized that I didn't have a cold, but I had been bitten by something—puppy love. Drew and I finally held hands. He was the first boy I kissed on the lips. He was the first boy that told me he loved me. Okay . . . his best friend told me while Drew sat stubbornly on the bottom of his pool with his hands pressed over his ears, but in the fourth grade that was good enough for me. We sealed our bond with a toy license plate that read:

Seek
N'
Carrington

We spent the summer playing tag and hide-and-seek. I was glad to see autumn so that I could watch Drew practice football. He was so little, so big, and so cute all at the same time. He waved at me as he ran around the track. I sat imagining the following year. Maybe our lockers would be next to each other, or we would have the same lunch. After practice one night, with the air filled with a slight chill yet warmed by the smell of burning leaves, Drew walked me to the top of the hill behind my house. The same hill he had sat perched on as he tried to get up the nerve to talk to me.

I floated into the kitchen with my cheek still warm from the shy kiss Drew had given me before he rode away on his bike across the baseball fields that separated our neighborhoods. Dinner was ready. Unlike usual, Dad wasn't watching the news. He always watched the news while he ate dinner. Not tonight, though. He had some news for me. He asked me to sit down at the table as my mother poured our tea; my dad silently buttered his rolls. Then he looked at me and told me we were moving from this small Midwestern town that was now my home to Las Vegas!

Gulp. Terror. Panic. Please, not again. I like my school. I just learned the neighborhood. I still have boxes in my closet from the last time. What about the shelves you said you would put up in my room? Can we take the cat? Omigosh! What about Drew? How are we supposed to grow up together? Go to our first dance? Get our driver's licenses together? Graduate together? Go to college? Get married? Have children? Grow old together?

Dad would never understand my disappointment. My world had just been turned upside down. Trying to explain would only start a fight. My dad would yell. My mom would cry. And it would be my fault. My face turned red as I smiled and quietly asked, "When do we leave?"

Drew wrote me three times before we lost touch. Six years later I called the old number I still had for him. Of course, he still had the same home, the same pool, the same yard. I found out that he went by Andy—Drew had been short for Andrew. He didn't play football anymore. He worked on cars. We wrote only twice before we lost touch again.

To this day, the sight of a roller-skating rink brings a smile to my face and my heart warms at the thoughts of my puppy love affair with Drew. I enjoy returning to those crisp evenings spent hiding together, riding bikes together, and just looking at each other. The memories are so vivid I can smell the grass and hear my neighbor's dog barking in the background. My own life is now full and sweet, but I still like to wrap myself in the warmth of his memory and the comfort it brings.

MICHELLE CARRINGTON

Be an answer to someone's prayer today.
C. YVONNE BROWN

GROOMING NISHA

*L*ast June, I had to give Nisha up. I knew she was going away for a good cause, but she took a piece of my heart with her, since I'd raised her from a puppy and watched her grow and mature.

It all started when I was on a summer camping trip with my family. Mom and I were walking on a trail and talking about finding an activity that I could get involved with to meet other kids and take on a responsibility. Mom said when she was young, she grew up in a "4-H family." All of her brothers and sisters belonged to a local 4-H group that she loved to bits.

The very next day, down by the lake, I saw a girl walking a puppy by the dock. The dog was wearing a green jacket. I had to find out why. I ran over and introduced myself. She told me her dog was a guide-dog puppy in training for the blind, and that she was doing this through her 4-H club in California. We talked a while longer, and then I ran to the cabin to tell my mom what I wanted to do.

Just before school started, we found out the name of the 4-H guide-dog group. After I filled out the application to be a guide-dog raiser, two leaders came to the house to interview me and my family. They wanted me to know what a big responsibility it is to raise a guide-dog puppy, and I assured them that I would do a great job.

We got a call in January that our puppy was coming soon—a female yellow lab. I could barely wait. When Dad and I picked her up, I melted. She was the cutest, prettiest dog I'd ever seen. From the moment I saw her, I knew she was going to be the best guide dog ever.

"Her name is Nisha," the trainer said. *Nisha,* I thought. We'd all been guessing what her name might be, and we loved the sound of Nisha. I smiled and hugged her tight.

When I started working with Nisha, I learned right away how intelligent dogs are. Guide-dog puppies seem to know that they are special and were born to do special work. As a puppy raiser, your main job is to love the puppy, teach them basic house rules, and socialize them—by exposing them to different situations and taking them to as many different places as you can. Nisha loved to ride in the car, and she loved to meet kids. I was allowed to take her anywhere a trained guide dog could go, including in stores, on the bus, and to school.

Nisha had Groucho Marx eyebrows. She had a way of cocking her head and wiggling her eyebrows that made me giggle. Nisha was also a good listener. Whenever I felt I needed to talk to someone, Nisha was always there. She loved to get her belly rubbed. I'd sit on the floor, and she'd come up to me and do a somersault between my legs.

As the year slipped by, Nisha bonded with the whole family, and we knew the day was coming when she'd have to go back for an intensive, five-month guide-dog training, the last month on-site with her new partner.

When it was time, we took her on her last car ride with us, and I dropped her off with the campus trainer. I gave her a long goodbye hug. As the staff member took her down the hall to the kennel, she looked back at me for a second as the door closed behind her. She was a bit confused, and I was very sad, but at the same time, I knew she was going to help someone. That night I cried in bed while I held her blanket—the one she used to sleep on next to my bed. The next morning, I woke up to the sound of rain, not the wet, warm licks from Nisha.

Five months went by, and along the way I got news that Nisha was passing each of the five phases she needed to in order to become a trained guide dog. In mid-May, I received the official letter that announced Nisha was to graduate as a working guide, and that she would be placed with a blind woman named Audrey. I was invited to present Nisha to Audrey at the graduation ceremony.

My family and I got up early to drive the two hours to the campus. I was so excited to see Nisha again! I wondered how much she'd changed. We went to the dormitory to wait. When they brought Nisha out, she looked the same—just a little bit bigger. She still had that reddish, golden color that made her so pretty. She was very happy to see us. Nisha looked more regal than I remembered her being. We got to meet Audrey before the ceremony, and we could all tell how much she and Nisha loved each other.

We learned Audrey was seventy-two years old and a bookkeeper at a bowling alley in a town near Seattle. We laughed and told Audrey that a bowling alley was about the only place I hadn't taken Nisha. Audrey told us she took Nisha to one during her month-end training, and Nisha loved it!

Before graduation, I stood in a single file line with eleven other puppy raisers. By our side, on leash, were our dogs. Audrey and the other graduates sat up on stage. One of the school's trainers welcomed everyone in the overflow audience and gave a short speech. Then, one by one, the graduates stood, and their puppy raiser walked their dog up on stage and handed off the leash. Each dog knowingly sat and waited for their next command. There wasn't a dry eye in the place. Each graduate joked and reminisced about their trying month as they learned to become one with their dogs and how they fell in love with them in the process. When it was my turn, Audrey thanked me for raising Nisha. It felt so good to know I'd played a part to help Audrey "see."

It was time to go home again, and I gave Nisha and Audrey one more hug. Audrey told me to consider her like a grandma, and that she'd write and send pictures of Nisha. As we left, I looked back and Nisha was looking straight at me—then she looked up at Audrey. She knew her job, and I knew they'd make a great team.

It's been a few weeks since graduation, and now I have a new handful. Norway is her name—and with my help, she is going to make someone else feel very happy and free.

KIRSTEN SNYDER

If I had never met him
I would have dreamed him into being.
ANZIA YEZIERSKA

AN ANGEL IN DISGUISE

Danny and I spent the hot Louisiana summer together at church camp where we worked as counselors when we were both nineteen. He was kind and gentle. We made plans for our future as young people often do. He was going to be doctor, and I, a nurse. It all fit together so nicely. I was going to transfer to the college he attended at the end of the fall semester. We had it all figured out—or so I thought.

During the last week of camp, he began to count down the hours to a surprise he had in store for me that weekend. "Only fifty hours!" he chimed. Thursday came. "Shelly, only twenty-four more hours!" This would be our first official date after working together all summer. We hopped in his car, and we started the evening by going out to eat. We left the restaurant just as the sun was beginning to set.

When we got back in his car, he didn't want me to see where we were going. Danny informed me he'd have to blindfold me before we could go any farther. Laughing, we could only imagine what it looked like for anyone driving by! We drove for a long while before he stopped his truck. He gave me his hand, and we stepped out into the night air. He led me through a black forest, illuminated only by the light of the moon. Sitting beside me on the ground, he said a quick prayer asking God to let this be the most perfect night that either of us would ever experience.

As I opened my eyes, the scene before me was breathtaking. Danny had brought me to the prayer garden. It was a sacred and special place at camp surrounded by water, ferns, flowers, and trees. We sat close together beside the lake under a full moon as the light from our small campfire expelled a soft light on the six-foot cross positioned in front of us across the water.

We held each other close, spoke in hushed voices, and cried from sheer reverence as we asked that God's will be done in our lives. We talked and dreamed for hours. At the end of the evening, we gazed up through the small clearing of pines into the beautiful night sky, and a meteor sailed by—as though God was running his finger, like a signature, across our little piece of heaven. It was the perfect ending to a perfect night.

My parents had invited Danny to stay with us that last night before he returned home for school. Morning came, and we both dreaded saying goodbye. I began to cry and he hugged me tight, saying, "I don't want you to hurt." But I was. My heart was breaking. "I wish I didn't have to go," Danny whispered. I wished he didn't either.

He stood in my front yard and his eyes—dark, mysterious, penetrating—shone brightly, yet I saw in them a strange sadness. His hair glistened as golden strands illuminated the light that seemed to encircle his head. I remember his hands—soft, clean, uncallused, with long, thin fingers. Danny looked at me in a way he had never looked before and then whispered, "Shelly, I'm really going to miss you. Please don't ever forget me."

Never smiling, he grabbed my hands and asked me to pray for him to make it home safely. With that, he gave me a last kiss, put on his helmet, climbed on his motorcycle, and rode away. I watched as he drove out of my sight and out of my life, never to return again.

Feeling confused at his peculiar goodbye, I went back into the house with a heavy heart. On the table lay a note Danny had written for me to discover after he'd gone. It read, "Pray for us" and referred me to a Bible verse: *Trust in the Lord with all your heart and lean not on your own understanding. In all your ways acknowledge Him and He shall direct your paths.* That was at 11:00 A.M. In less than an hour, my world collapsed. Forty-five minutes after leaving my house, Danny was involved in an accident that took his life.

Life after that held little meaning for me. My pain was so great and my sorrow unsurpassed. I became so desperate in my grief that I asked God to let me dream of Danny. My prayers were frequently answered, and after one of those dreams, it felt like we'd spent time together saying things we needed to say and tying up loose ends. We even said goodbye in one of those dreams, and over time I slowly began to heal.

Six years have passed since Danny died. Not long ago, I was playing outside with my dog well after dark. I looked up toward the heavens, and my mind immediately raced back to the one thing Danny had asked me to do, "Shelly, please don't ever forget me." My heart once again became heavy as I recalled all my despair that echoed Danny's name. I felt shame, because it had been a while since I'd thought of him. Loneliness and pain began to swell like waves inside my chest. I prayed to God to bring me Danny one last time. I'd forgotten the sound of his voice, the distinct color of his hair, and the kindness in his eyes.

Less than a week passed, and I once again forgot about Danny and my prayer. I threw myself back into my work and my hurried everyday life. On Sunday, at church, I sat in the next-to-last pew. When the service started, I hardly noticed the man who took a seat behind me. During a song of fellowship, I turned to greet the stranger behind me. My heart stopped for a moment, and I felt a heavenly warmth envelop my body. He reached and took my hand and smiled very slowly, as if to say, "It's okay." Then he winked. His eyes were more beautiful than I remembered. His hair still had touches of gold. I felt myself smile as I remembered my prayer from the week before. He rose from his seat. I gazed lovingly and in utter amazement as he moved closer to grasp my hand. Before he sat back down, I saw his hands— beautiful hands—perfect doctor's hands—Danny's hands.

I fought hard to hold back my tears. I couldn't wait to talk with him at the end of the service, but when I turned back toward him, he was gone. Just as gently and quietly as he appeared, he disappeared. He spoke to no one, and no one had seemed to notice him but me.

Back at home, I told Mom what happened. She thought for a moment and then asked, "What is the date today?" I had to think for a moment. "It's the fourteenth," I answered. My eyes filled with tears—Danny had died on the fourteenth. He had always come to me in dreams on this date.

That afternoon, I went to his grave for the last time. Suddenly, his epitaph had even more significance: *An Angel in Disguise.*

SHELLY CLARK

A MAGICAL MOMENT

*I*n life, one event may take on a special significance and become permanently etched in our minds.

One such magical moment stands out for me. I was sitting in the lobby of the Contemporary Hotel at Disney World. I was thirteen. My dad, my stepmom, and her parents were shopping for souvenirs in the stores nearby. All around, people were milling about, sending a comfortable hum of voices through the spacious atrium. The sun bathed the air with a yellow glow, complementing the lush, tropical greenery. The monorails glided and stopped, one after another, and a peacefulness settled on the late hours of a busy day.

I was alone on a bench, watching the people. We'd been at the Magic Kingdom all day, and I was tired. I noticed a boy—a really cute boy—who was about my age. He was watching me. Standing, leaning on a pole just watching me. He had soft brown hair, and he was smiling. He made my heart flutter.

He surprised me by walking over and sitting down next to me. Close. He smelled good, so good that I've always wondered what that smell was exactly. A nervous wave washed over me as I struggled awkwardly to make conversation.

"Hi," I said.

"Hey," he said.

A long pause. We both shifted uneasily on the bench.

"What kind of cologne are you wearing?" I finally asked.

"I dunno," he said indifferently. "It's my father's—musk or something."

He touched the balloon I was holding. A blue Mickey Mouse balloon, I'll never forget it. Then he leaned over and kissed me, a warm, gentle kiss that made me dizzy and fuzzy-headed.

In that moment, I felt independent—like being "all grown up." Perhaps that kiss sparked the woman inside me. I tasted freedom and felt the soft flutter of romance in my heart for the first time.

That was the end of the magical boy. The next thing I knew, my stepmom demanded to know why I kissed a stranger in the lobby of a hotel after being alone for less than five minutes. I don't blame her for being embarrassed. After all, I did it right in front of her parents. Truth was, I really didn't know why or how I came to be sitting there kissing a stranger. I just knew I liked it, and that I was in a lot of trouble.

I spent the ride home in the backseat of the car—my head resting against the window, gazing out quietly, while holding my Mickey Mouse balloon close to my face. The smell of that balloon kept me with him all the way home. And the feeling of his kiss stayed fresh on my heart.

I saved the balloon for many years. I don't know if it was special to me because of the boy, or because it represented a time in my life when I gained a new sense of independence, a magical coming of age.

Almost twenty years later, I found myself at the Columbia restaurant in Tampa sitting next to a man whom I found to be intriguing. As I leaned closer to him, I noticed he smelled fantastic—a fragrance I remembered from long ago. I asked him what he was wearing. "I don't know," he said, "I can't remember the name." I looked deep into his eyes and wondered.

CHERIE PEDÉ

Don't compromise yourself. You are all you've got.
JANIS JOPLIN

BE CAREFUL
WHAT YOU ASK FOR

"**F**ind me a guy," I said to Kara one evening as I plopped down on her bed. She just laughed at me. We often teased that of all the girls in our sorority sophomore class, I was the one who didn't need to depend on a man and was going to college for an education.

Not long after that, I met Ryan. We hung out for hours when we first met, talking about everything under the sun. The best part was that he found me fascinating. Ryan envied the fact that I was career-oriented, was a campus leader, and had strong family ties. From that day on, we were almost inseparable. People described us at the perfect couple, and for a while we were. But that was also a problem. To me, Ryan was just a college boyfriend. I didn't see him as "the one," nor did I see him in my future. These feelings surfaced about six months into our relationship. While visiting Ryan one day in his hometown during the summer, I suggested we go to the mall. I'd been searching for an everyday ring. He told me that he'd found the perfect one, and he had a salesperson pull out an expensive diamond ring. I just about died! I had too many plans, dreams, and goals for myself. I wanted to get my career started and become

financially stable on my own before I ever thought about marriage.

We began to argue after we left the mall. I said, "I can't believe
you put me on the spot like that! At this point, I don't see us
being married." Ryan seemed devastated by this news. He was
sure we'd marry someday. Then his violent temper surfaced. He
shattered the windshield of my car.

I decided to end our relationship when school began, but I
was caught in his web of sweet talk, despite the frightening side
of him I'd now seen. We left it that we would date other people
but still see each other. I got to know a new group of kids for a
few weeks, and one of the guys invited me out to a movie. To
this day, it was one of the best dates I've ever been on. He was a
perfect gentleman, opening doors for me wherever we went and
holding my hand when we walked. On our way home, I thanked
him for a great evening. "You should always be treated like gold,"
he said matter-of-factly. While saying goodnight, he whispered,
"Michelle, deep down you know you can do better than Ryan."
We parted on that thought.

When I got to my room, Ryan had left a ton of messages. His
fraternity was partying that night and a few of my girlfriends
were going. I decided to join them and wound up confessing to
Ryan that I'd just returned from a date. He went crazy. Scared by
the way he was acting, I got up to leave his room. I got to the
door and he slammed it shut, pinning me against it. I'd never
been so frightened in my life. The look in his eyes was what
scared me the most. Finally I got a hand free and punched him in
his side. He let go of me, and I ran out of the house. Over the
next couple of days, he called, sent cards, and fed me more
lines—and I fell for them again. It *seemed* as if he'd changed.

The physical violence became more frequent, and I withdrew
from society. My secret life had begun. My friends tried to help
me, but I kept turning them away, making excuses for Ryan's behavior and not admitting the abuse. My boss began to reprimand

me because I was consistently late, my grades had fallen, and I was losing too much weight. The relationship began affecting my family life as well. We fought just about every time I called home. Along the way, I lost a best friend, a roommate, and my sister. Weary of the Michelle-and-Ryan saga, none of them wanted anything to do with me.

Ryan and I were at his apartment cooking dinner one night when I told him, "I'm taking someone else to my sorority ball. I'm sorry, but we are just too unstable right now." He got up from the kitchen table and said, "If I can't have you, no one else can!" As scared as I was, I stood my ground. We wound up getting into the most intense fight, beating each other with everything and anything we had, including dinner. Because I was actually defending myself this time, he got madder. He began hitting harder and restraining me more. At one point—like an out-of-body experience—I remember watching myself fighting with him, I was viewing the fight from the kitchen doorway. I have no recollection of feeling any pain. I just kept saying to myself, *Michelle, you're better than this. Your parents raised you better than this. How mad would your father be if he knew you were in this situation?* Coming back from my dreamlike state, I ended the fight and left.

Depression settled in, and I began avoiding people. A professor asked me to stay after class one day and said, "Michelle, I'm not going to ask what's going on in your life, but I will let you know that you are not yourself. You've been late to class, don't turn your assignments in on time, and you don't participate anymore. I'm noticing these things, and can't help but wonder where your enthusiasm went." I left without saying a word. I could no longer keep my secret life hidden.

I began searching for the old me that summer, and Ryan and I rarely spoke. I started dating again, hanging out with old friends, and trying to take better care of myself. Ryan found out that I was seeing someone else. He broke into my apartment, trashed my room, and left an awful note behind. My roommate came with me and we filed a police report; the officer said he would put the fear of God in Ryan, which is just what he did. We've been apart ever since.

After a lot of soul searching, talking, and reuniting with friends and family, I found my old self. When I faced the truth and shared out loud that Ryan had abused me, my secret life came to an end. And his power over me stopped.

I look at my life today, and I feel grateful. Using joy as my compass, I'm strong, independent, and goal-oriented once again. You have to be careful what you ask for. Just "finding a guy" was not what I needed. From now on, I will only spend time with a man who treats me like gold!

MICHELLE THOMAS

MY TRUE LOVE

Tiny raindrops slid down the window as the wind whispered through the eaves. I slid a Brian McKnight CD into the stereo and set to work. I sorted through the skirts and dresses hanging in the closet, discarding several in a large plastic bag. I then tackled the clutter at the bottom and tossed out old tennis shoes, a pair of ancient pink slippers, and the peach-colored flats that I wore to the seventh-grade dance. From under a battered backpack in the corner, I unearthed my "memory box" filled with old photographs and a shriveled corsage from the junior prom, along with scribbled notes and love letters tied with white satin ribbons. I sat on the floor, lifted the lid, and traveled to the past.

Jimmy's sweet young face smiled up at me from a yellowed photo that was taken at a neighborhood block party. He lived next door and always shared his candy with me. He had a gap between his front teeth, and he continuously wore a Pittsburgh Pirate's cap with the bill tilted over his left eye. We were inseparable that long ago summer, but what could I possibly know of love back then? I was only five.

Robin was so cute with his dark auburn hair and sprinkling of freckles over the bridge of his nose. He was the first guy to bring me flowers, a handful of drooping daisies with the roots still attached, and the first to ask for a date. There was one small problem. The movie theater was ten blocks away, and neither of us was old enough to cross the street.

I had a heart-wrenching, unrequited "crush" on Gary for three long years. I'm not sure what it was about him that was so attractive. He wasn't the most handsome or the most popular guy in school. There was just something about him. . . . He played the drums. I loved it when he practiced on the wooden desktop with two pencils, but it drove our geometry teacher *nuts!*

Dale, the clown of the ninth grade, was in my life for a brief time when I was fifteen. He was very tall and as thin as spaghetti, and he could always make me laugh. Unfortunately, he used to bathe in his father's Old Spice cologne. The awful smell and his groping, octopus hands eventually drove me away.

I thought fondly of Ronnie. He was very sensitive and truly adorable with black, curly hair tied at the nape of his neck and dark eyes framed by long, thick lashes. His smile melted my heart, but sadly, he was not very bright. I sincerely hope that he found a rich woman to take care of him.

The mere sight of Bob took my breath away and made my knees quiver. At seventeen, I was sure he was *the one.* Bob was incredibly handsome, with hair the color of wheat and big blue eyes. Alas, Bob had a heart of stone and was hell-bent on breaking more hearts than Leonardo DiCaprio. What I felt wasn't love at all. It was pure lust.

So many memories passed through my mind. Some brought a smile to my face and some made me a little sad. After lovingly examining each, I tucked them away, and their images blurred and grew dim.

As I bundled the photos and retied the ribbons, another image drifted into my thoughts. This mental picture has blossomed from a vague concept to an almost tangible entity, which grows more defined with each passing year, yet the face is still indistinguishable. I try to visualize his features, but they're just beyond my grasp. Nevertheless, a certain sweetness and intelligence is discernible, and I can clearly see what's in his heart. He's warm and romantic, sensitive to my moods, and mindful of my feelings, and he will support me in whatever I endeavor. He'll bring

UNFORGETTABLE BEAUTY

After Beauty died, our neighbors often said they missed seeing her wiggle through the bushes, searching out an early morning rub of ear or pat of head. The mailman stopped me too to ask why Beauty no longer barked a greeting through the mail slot. Those close friends who had known Beauty since she was a puppy sent condolence cards on the loss of a pet.

But no mailman's kindness, no neighbors' comments or friends' cards, were able to stop the swell of sorrow in our home after Beauty died. For days after our loss, we could not look at one another without crying, our arms reaching to one another again and again in search of comfort. Meals were eaten in almost total silence. Sibling quarrels vanished into thin air. I could not remove Beauty's feeding dishes from the spot where they had been filled daily for over twelve years. Beauty's death was especially hard on her master, our son Eric, whose bed Beauty had shared from her puppy days.

It was Eric who had found his beloved Beauty in a coma and awakened us around 2:00 A.M. with his shouts. "Beauty, Beauty, c'mon, girl, wake up! Wake up!" We flew out of bed and ran into Eric as he was running into our room shouting, "Mom! Dad! It's Beauty! I think she's dying!"

By then, our daughters, hearing the hullabaloo, were up too, and the five of us crowded around Eric's bed, now touching Beauty, now hugging one another, wondering what to do.

me flowers and make me laugh, and he'll love music as much as I do. He'll be generous, kind, and compassionate, and he *won't* wear Old Spice.

Although we've yet to meet, I've no doubt that I'll recognize him. There will be *something* about him. He'll take my breath away, make my knees quiver, and his smile will melt my heart.

MARGARET J. (MIMI) POPP

Should we call the vet? Did the humane society have an emergency room, a hospice? Should we kneel down, stand up, get dressed, stay in our pajamas? And what about Beauty? Would rigor mortis set in and make it impossible to lift her? Beauty was a good-sized dog, a 70-pound German shorthair pointer. We all knew for some time that she was on in years and would not last long. Now her death was imminent. It could happen, we realized, within the next hour or two.

"Let's get her off the bed," my husband said. "Maybe we could wrap her up and get her down to the front porch at least." Gently, then, the men in the family wrapped Beauty in the bed quilt and made their way with her down the steps. The girls and I followed the procession, weeping with every step we took.

"Her heart's still beating," Eric said, as he settled on the porch floor, cradling Beauty in his arms. The moan of foghorns coming from the harbor on Lake Michigan became a dirge, echoing our sorrow through the darkness. Four of us could not speak. Only Eric found voice enough to comfort his Beauty, as she lay dying in his arms.

One by one, we stole away from this young man and his dog, knowing his voice was the one Beauty awoke to each morning, the last she heard each night. We knew he would recount for her all the times they had played a game of fetch on the beaches of Lake Michigan, the early-morning paper route they had shared for many years, the romps through the fields of Door County, and the joys of growing up together, a boy and his dog. We knew he would thank her too for her faithfulness, her trust in us, and her guarding ways when the girls were little. We left Eric to comfort her as she had once comforted us by her profuse welcome each time we came home from work or school.

Beauty died in Eric's arms around five in the morning.

"Oh, my Beauty, oh, my Beauty," the girls cried over and over when we woke them to say that she was gone.

One night two months later, I tucked the girls under their quilts, and they asked if they could have another dog. Without my answering, they began tossing names back and forth.

"How about Beauty II?"

"No, no, I think it should be Beast. You know, like in Beauty and the Beast."

"Maybe *two* dogs—Beauty *and* the Beast."

Excellent idea, I thought. It would probably take two balls of fur to replace what a beauty we once had.

JEAN JEFFREY GIETZEN

Friends are angels who lift us to our feet
when our wings have trouble remembering how to fly.
ANONYMOUS

AISHA, MARCUS, AND ADRIAN

*A*t eighteen years of age, with fifteen years of schooling behind me, I've gotten drunk from champagne once, skinny-dipped three times, and been truly afraid for my life twice—once when I sucked in too much seawater somewhere off the coast of Florida, and once during my junior year in high school when my father saw my physics grade. Love was not of great importance in the life of someone who was mainly concerned with her grades, her friends, and her weekend agenda.

I met Marcus at the end of the first month of college my freshman year. I don't remember exactly when or how, but all of a sudden he appeared in my dorm room and it seemed he had been there before. He was my friend for the first few weeks. He listened with a sympathetic ear when I had guy troubles, made me laugh, and frequently accompanied me to eat, a prospect that becomes daunting when one is a freshman and facing the cafeteria alone. And then one rainy night on our way to dinner, we shared an umbrella. His arm curved comfortably around my shoulders, and I knew I wanted him to kiss me. We returned to my room later that night, watched the city lights blur in the rain outside my window, and as they say, the rest was history.

Marcus was my first real boyfriend and soon became my first love. Two months after we met, I was designing our wedding invitations in my head during computer science class. I knew that he was the one for me. I have always been a planner—from my high school prom date to my degree requirements to the color of my future bridesmaids' dresses. And Marcus fit right in. I was convinced that my first love was to be my last. He wanted to be a radiologist. I was going to be a lawyer. We were going to be *The Cosby Show.*

I fell in love with him holding my hand. I fell in love with falling asleep in his arms. My parents drove up to school to meet him, and we all went to eat at a Thai restaurant. All he had to do was pull out my mother's chair for her. She gave me a wink and later, during dessert, whispered to me that he was a keeper. During Thanksgiving break, we went to the mall together. I glanced at a black pearl and diamond ring underneath the counter, and minutes later it was slipped onto the index finger of my right hand. One late night in December, I was on Chapter 12 in my psychology textbook at 2:00 A.M. with four more chapters to go. I looked up from reading about the learning patterns of chimpanzees, and there was Marcus standing in my door with coffee and a single peach rose. When he flew in to see me during Christmas break, I was delighted to find that he even hit it off with my best friend Adrian.

Adrian has lived across the street from me for ten years. We've been best friends since the fourth grade. She helped me name my pet guinea pig. We were in the same Girl Scout troop. She let me borrow her jewelry when I couldn't find the right piece to complement an outfit, and she helped undo my braids at night, a process that can take hours. We have fallen asleep on each other's couches together too many times to count. She and Marcus got along from the beginning. They both had the same sense of humor and delighted in teasing me. They both loved video games and cartoons. And Adrian knew I was happy. That was what mattered the most to her.

Then, in the beginning of March, Marcus and I went for a walk on a foggy Connecticut night, and he told me he had fallen out of love with me. I was devastated. Adrian was on the phone with me for an hour that night trying to convince me there would be others and that I shouldn't hide in my room for the rest of the year. I could not look at Marcus the entire week before spring break, and during vacation I took my bleeding heart down to my grandmother's house in Florida. She cooked me banana fritters and knocked my hand away from the phone every time she had the suspicion I was picking it up to call Marcus. Slowly, I started to heal. After I returned from Florida, however, there was a message waiting for me. I was still in love, and less than a week after we got back to school, Marcus and I were an item again.

Thus began a series of makeups and breakups. I lost count of how many times we'd get frustrated and angry and say it was over. We couldn't agree on anything. Choosing a video to rent was a chore. Deciding where to eat, an argument. We even fought over what music to play while we kissed. And we were bored without each other. We kept coming back together because of what we thought was a desperate need for each other. Now I know it was more like loneliness and lust. It was nice for a while. But we soon figured out that we were the two most opposite people alive. The love and the need we thought we had became tearful fights and stony silences. And it hurt.

Adrian was never a silent bystander. I was so wrapped up with Marcus that my phone calls and e-mails to her became less and less frequent. And then I'd get a message, "Where have you been? What has that boy done to you? Call me." And she had no problem letting me know that she thought Marcus was no longer healthy for me. But I ignored her because only I knew what was best for me.

I'm not saying everything between Marcus and I became hostile. When he kissed me, everything was right. He knew how to hold me, knew that I liked it when he cupped the side of my face, knew I would sigh when he traced my collarbones.

But in the end, I loved myself more than his kisses. I adored the way he held me, but it didn't make up for the tears, the arguments, the you-said-you'd-calls, and the why-don't-you-love-me-anymores. I had to make a choice.

The person I ran to when I broke up with my first love is no surprise. It was summer by then, and in tears, I ran across the street and threw myself down on Adrian's bed. Two days later we watched the Fourth of July fireworks over the East River in Manhattan together.

And a little while later, in my heart, I said goodbye to Marcus. I learned about the power of first love from the boy at school and about the staying power of friendship from the girl across the street.

AISHA D. GAYLE

III
GROWING PAINS

Pain is important: how we evade it, how we succumb to it,
how we deal with it, how we transcend it.

AUDRE LORDE

SOUTHWICK'S SWEATSHIRT

The sound of his voice made me jump. "Would you like a sweatshirt?" His breath was uncomfortably close and warm on my ear. My quizzical look met his impatient one. "Would you like a sweatshirt?" he asked again.

"Um, uh, sure." Automatic and unchecked, the words stumbled from my lips. In sudden realization of what I had replied, panic set in. "No! I don't want a sweatshirt. I'm just a freshman. You shouldn't be lending me anything." Something blue and warm was thrust into my arms. My cheeks burned as a wave of hot embarrassment swept over me. It couldn't be helped now. I couldn't just hand it back. Clumsily, I pulled the big blue mess over my head. I glanced down at the bold white words that announced, "David Southwick/Senior Class" across my chest. Oh, how I wished he had never asked if I was cold.

The more I thought about it, the worse it got. He asked if I was cold because I was shivering. He was probably annoyed that I had come to marching rehearsal unprepared and without a sweatshirt of my own. But I did have one, only it was out of reach on the sidelines of the football field. In anguish, I yearned for the hour to end, so I could be rid of this fuzzy complication. I was pleased he had thought of me, but much more I wished he had never noticed. Oh, what was his girlfriend thinking? What was everyone else thinking? I wasn't flirting with him. It was an accident!

The director's eyes were upon me. "Come on, now, let's keep up the intensity!" he bellowed.

Certain the comment was directed at me, I strove to concentrate on the drill. "Calm down," I scolded myself. "I'll just have to wear it. There's nothing I can do but wait this out. In a few minutes marching band practice will end, and we will be dismissed. I can return his sweatshirt, and it'll all be over."

I felt uncomfortably hot and self-conscious. My mind wandered and I struggled to hold my focus. Time crept. Every agonizing minute was an eternity, but practice ended at last. Dismissal came. With forced slow steps, I fought down the urge to bolt from the football field.

I tore off the sweatshirt, trying not to seem frantic. Picking David out, I thrust the blue wad at him. "Thanks," I mumbled smiling weakly, eagerly handing it over.

His mind was obviously on something else. "Oh, you're welcome." He scooped up his sweatshirt and walked away without a backward glance.

My breath returning in sudden gasps of freedom, I turned away trying to shake off the weirdness. "He took it back and didn't think anything of it. No one did," I convinced myself. Finally, I could relax. With a small laugh of relief, I picked up my own sweatshirt and walked away.

BRIANNA MAHIN-AYERS

ENHANCED WITH LACE

W*e all have life experiences we would prefer to* forget. One of these was a particularly traumatic one that occurred my freshman year of high school in PE.

PE meant mandatory communal showers. Until this time, possessing a well-endowed female figure was of no significance to me. That this was a primary concern among my fellow students became apparent when I came upon a discussion in the hall between two older girls. One was standing against the wall looking down her chest to the floor. They were comparing how much of their feet was visible. Apparently whether one could see one's feet and to what degree they were obscured by one's bosom was their criterion for an acceptable teenage female body. I could look straight down and see my feet with no interference. Consequently, I spent the better part of the school year hiding among hanging clothes and dashing with Olympic speed in and out of the shower room.

Finally the embarrassment became too much. I went home one afternoon and told my mother, "I need to buy a bra."

"What for?" she asked.

Standing there crushed, I answered, "Because all the other girls have one."

Mother stood silent for a moment, then said, "We'll go shopping Saturday."

Satisfied I would soon walk among the proud, I busied myself with assigned chores and homework.

On Saturday, we parked downtown and walked to Eiband's. As we entered, I thought, "I shall come out an entirely different person never to be ridiculed again." Little did I know.

We rode to the second floor in the antique wire-cage elevator. We turned left and walked to a display case containing beautiful lacy undergarments. I tried to look mature and knowing, but knew I was only fooling myself.

"May I help you?"

I looked up and felt instant relief. This was someone new who hadn't known me since I was a baby.

"Yes," said Mother. "We're looking for a bra."

The saleslady glanced from her to me and back again. "Of course. What size?"

"Well," Mother hesitated, "I really don't know. It's for my daughter."

"Certainly." The lady smiled and, turning to me, said, "If the young lady will come with me to the dressing room, I'll measure her."

I groaned inwardly. Couldn't she tell just by looking? She asked me to remove my blouse and discreetly measured me over my slip. She stood there a moment and said, "Hmmm." Then smiled and said, "I'll be right back."

The little blue overstuffed chair next to the mirror looked inviting, so I sat. Conversation filtered through the louvered door.

"I'm afraid we haven't anything quite right for your daughter," the lady said. (Training bras hadn't been invented yet.)

Mother sighed loudly. "I didn't think so, but would you mind letting her try on the smallest size you have?"

"Of course not," the lady said.

After a few minutes of sounds of drawers opening and closing and paper rustling, the saleslady returned to the dressing room.

"Would you like to try on any of these?" she asked enthusiastically as she held up an array of cotton bras daintily enhanced with lace.

I decided to try them all. She left the room and left me to the contortionist act of hooking the band in the back. I became more and more discouraged as I tried each one on. They felt awful and constricting. Now I knew how a horse in harness must feel. Not only that, my cups didn't runneth over. For that matter, they weren't even half full. A knock on the door startled me.

"Do you need any help?" came the gentle question, behind which I read much understanding.

"No, ma'am, thank you, I've decided to take the white one and the blue one."

I opened the door a crack and handed the bras through. Tears filled my eyes as I finished dressing. There had been no magic, and I wasn't any different.

As we stepped out into the Saturday afternoon sun, I began to feel my life could go no way but down.

"We have a few minutes," Mother said. "How about a frosted root beer?"

Ah, Mother truly knew the direct route to my heart.

Monday came too soon. I wore my new white cotton bra, which my clothes duly squashed. After PE I tried to get undressed for the mandatory shower as quickly and quietly as possible. I was about to breathe a sigh of relief when, "Look, she has a bra!"

Amid squeals of laughter came "I don't know why, she doesn't have anything to put in it." More laughter. I showered and dressed, knowing it wouldn't take long for the word to spread.

Toward the end of the school year, I discovered that students in the band were exempt from PE. I became possessed with a burning desire to be in the band. I made an appointment to speak with the band director. When he learned of my music background, he readily accepted me into the group.

With the success of being accepted into the band, I thought all my troubles were over. Little did I know. I had to be measured for a uniform. That wouldn't have been so bad, except the students, male and female, were assembled in the same room and their measurements called out.

The dreaded moment arrived and my name was called. I bravely walked up and inwardly steeled myself for raucous jest and laughter. The measurer called, "Twenty-eight, eighteen, twenty-eight." I held my breath. Nothing. No snide remarks. Nothing. The next person's name was called and I moved on. I gathered my schoolbooks and walked out of the band hall with back straight and head held high. Maybe life wasn't so bad after all.

JUNETTE KIRKHAM WOLLER

PRETTY ENOUGH

A lot of things were going on in my life. When I was a teenager, I did anything that would bring my mother to tears, and so I was braless, had a yard's worth of hair constantly falling in front of my face, and wore dirty clothes. I dismissed concern for my own physical beauty—nothing could be more meaningless to me. No makeup touched my face, no scissors touched my hair, and aside from the fact that all my clothes were black and easily matched, I made no fashion statement.

I was totally unlike my very blond best friend, who could find her way through a cosmetics store blindfolded—except that feat would prevent her from following her reflection as she passed the mirrors.

The reason Jennifer was friends with me at all was because she was in love with my older brother. We had gone through high school together, but members of the twirlers do not socialize with members of the poetry club. The loathing was mutual—we were both snobs of our own sort.

We first spoke when she tailed my brother home from school in her new Mustang. Meeting her that day as I washed my mongrel (part German shepherd, part coyote) in the driveway, it was immediately clear that there was something about her that I liked. For all her pomp and vanity, she was also brutally honest about her feelings and her needs. I respected that. It made her more *earthy*. Unfortunately, she could be *too* honest.

That year, the year that Jennifer and I went to the fateful Saturday night movie together, I was in love with another very evolved individual, a young man of great insight and intellect, who had dumped me that morning. Since my brother was away, Jennifer had agreed to be my date for the evening.

We went to the movies at the mall and discovered a long line. We were both self-conscious about being out together on date night. After looking around to see if she knew anyone in line, and finding no one, Jennifer allowed herself to make discreet conversation with me, the badly dressed girl who just happened to be standing next to her.

We had already discussed my grief during the morning and the afternoon, and I had promised her I wouldn't cry again until we had returned home from the movie. But here in line, there really would have been no point trying to talk about anything else. She knew my grief consumed me.

"I have to tell you," she began. "I saw him with another girl yesterday. He had his arm around her waist, and they looked like they were really together." So after a day of reluctant shoulder loaning, she at last got that out.

Naturally I was on the verge of self-destruction, but I managed to peep, "What did she look like?"

"Well," Jennifer said, "she had red hair. It was pulled back tight. And a cute little figure. Pretty, really." She was straight, with absolutely no hint of compassion.

Busting out of my vulnerability and now unable to contain my deepest concern, I had to ask, "Well, was she prettier than me?"

Here was her chance of redemption. I had handed her the easiest and quickest opportunity to help me through this blow. But alas, she was true to form. Jennifer looked at me, smiled that condescending—I was a twirler and you weren't—smile and said, "Well, you're not a *pretty* girl."

I'm not quite sure how she got home from the mall that night. And to this day, I don't remember what movie I missed. I don't even remember why I loved that boy. But her statement taught me something very important about myself. I have never forgotten what she said, and I can still hear her breathy, just-stating-the-facts tone. But every time I pass my face in the mirror, or look at it in a picture, I no longer believe her words.

I know I blamed her for a lot that went wrong in my life after that night—my insecurities, my subservient behaviors, and my endless search for beauty. I allowed her comment to control me for a very long time—until I was forced to grow up and find my inner beauty, release the burden of her perception, and just be me without the defiance.

Forced to create my own perception by the photographer at my wedding. Forced by the births of my sons. Forced by the fact that I no longer had time to think about makeup or clothes. And the only beautiful faces I cared about were those of my children.

I have no idea whatever happened to Jennifer. As it is, I barely have enough time to squeeze into my full, productive, often weary but splendid days, a *pretty enough* woman's life.

BETH SCHORR JAFFE

Truth is like an invisible warrior. It will save you from the battlefield.
IYANLA VANZANT

SNICKERS AND GRACE

*M*y fourth-grade teacher, Mrs. Huggins, was five feet two inches tall with short blond hair and a round face with a body to match. She smelled like Lemon Pledge. No real beauty, but when I think of loveliness, I always think of her.

In the summer before the fourth grade, my family and I went to Myrtle Beach, South Carolina, attended Dad's company picnic at the furniture plant, and went swimming at the city pool. So I wasn't very enthusiastic about our first all-too-familiar writing assignment back in school: "What I Did This Summer." That is until the Snickers bar entered the picture! The carrot dangled before us was this: Each of the six best essays won a huge Snickers bar. A devious plan was hatching in my head. No way could I just tell the humdrum story of an ordinary beach trip.

At church, I'd seen a poster on the wall promoting an upcoming gathering of Baptist missionaries in New Mexico. That was it! I would weave a tale about my trip there. And so my essay of lies began:

What I Did This Summer: This summer I went to Glorietta, New Mexico, to attend the conference of missionaries [lie # 1]. My mother took me shopping and bought me all new clothes for the trip [lie # 2]. My father arranged for me to fly on an airplane for the first time in my life [lie #3]. I stayed in the home of my aunt and uncle who are missionaries to Africa [another lie]. I saw the desert and cacti and coyotes [more lies]. On Wednesday evening I sang for the entire assembly, "I'll Tell the World That I'm a Christian" [I should have sung "Lying Eyes"]. I had a wonderful time. Maybe one day I'll be a missionary [fat chance of that, unless there is a need for converts to Liars Anonymous!].

I rewrote my essay three times and carefully packed my masterpiece in my book bag as if I were handling fine china. I could taste the sweet reward!

Five agonizing days passed before Mrs. Huggins announced with a grin, "I have chosen the six winners of our essay contest. Everyone did such a fine job that I found it difficult to decide." *(Yeah, yeah, I thought. Teachers always say that so the poor schmo who wrote the story about the zoo won't feel too bad.)*

"Now, before I go on," she continued, "I must tell you that winners will receive their candy after school today. But if you ride the bus, you must not eat your candy until you get home, and if you walk home, be sure to place your wrapper in a proper receptacle." *(OK, for pity sakes! I impatiently stewed. Just give me a cup to catch my drool!)*

Finally she stepped from behind her desk with six essays in her hand. I strained to see if anything in the stack of papers looked familiar, but she held them too closely to her breast. "The winners of the essay assignment are Paul George for his trip to the beach *(Totally boring, I thought)*, Amanda Jones for her trip to Gatlinburg, Tennessee *(What a joke, I mused)*, Willard Blevins for his trip to the railroad museum *(Maybe I aimed too high, I confidently chuckled)*, Becky Jarvis for her trip to see the Statue of Liberty *(Finally, some competition, I conceded)*, Peggy Moffet for her essay on what she did this summer in her own hometown

(That should have been about half a page), and . . . I bit my finger at the knuckle as she held the last paper. "And, the sixth and final winner is Dawn Spainhour for her trip to New Mexico!" *(Oh! Rapture! Ecstasy! She bought it!! Only two more hours and the Snickers is mine!)*

As I walked home, chocolate surrounded my mouth and covered the tips of my fingers. The error of my ways was replaced by the sweetness of the moment. The end did justify the means. I stopped by Mr. Cloer's market and disposed of the wrapper as carefully as a robber hiding his stash. The perfect crime!

I gave no more thought to my escapade. The week continued on rather uneventfully until Wednesday night, when we had supper in the fellowship hall at church. Sitting at a table covered with a red-checkered tablecloth, my family laughed, talked, and devoured chicken pie, green beans, macaroni and cheese, cobbler, and homemade rolls. One of our church members was on her way over to our table, and my life flashed before my eyes.

"Hi, Barbara," Mrs. Huggins said as she greeted my mother. "I know you must be so proud of this girl." As the blood drained from my face and acid rushed to my stomach, my eyes turned downward as the conversation continued. Why had I chosen tonight to sit next to my mother? There was no escape.

"Did Dawn tell you she won the essay contest at school?" Mrs. Huggins inquired. My mother looked at me, but I avoided all eye contact. "Why, no, she didn't," my mother responded. Mrs. Huggins dug my grave even deeper. "Well, she did, and she received a Snickers bar, too! I think it's wonderful that you and Jack let her go to Glorietta Conference Center and stay with her aunt and uncle. I don't believe I've ever heard you mention them before."

My mother clenched my arm with a death grip as she made my confession. "Mrs. Huggins," my mother carefully said through gritted teeth, "Dawn went to Myrtle Beach this summer." Hot tears rolled down my face as I continued to study the top of my shoes. "She didn't go to New Mexico, and furthermore, both her father and I are only children. She has no aunt or uncle. I have taught my daughter better than this."

The ride home from church was unbearable! Me in the car, sandwiched between my parents in the front seat, listening to Mom's tearful question, "How could you embarrass our family this way?" Then Dad chimed in, "Well, young lady, aren't you ashamed of yourself for making your mother cry?" *Yes,* I thought, *I'm sorry—I got caught!*—although this was not the time to answer rhetorical questions. *Was a Snickers worth all this sobbing, blaming, and grief?* I wondered. The answer came quickly, *Oh, yeah!*

The next morning, Mom and I stopped by Mr. Cloer's market to buy enough Snickers bars for my twenty-four classmates. The money came out of my meager 50-cent weekly allowance. I figured I wouldn't see money again until July Fourth! We entered the room, and Mrs. Huggins introduced my mother to the class. "Class, this is Mrs. Spainhour. She and Dawn have something to say to us today."

"My daughter, Dawn," Mom cleared her throat, "wrote an essay that won her a candy bar. But she lied and, therefore, did not deserve to win. Her dad and I have punished her *(Yeah,* I thought, *I hope the welts on my legs where I got a switching aren't showing!),* and she has paid for each of you to have a candy bar out of her allowance." The class sat strangely silent at this good news. I guess they'd figured out this was not a time for celebration. Mrs. Huggins helped me distribute the candy, then dismissed the class for recess and bade my mother goodbye.

Mrs. Huggins called me to her side, "Dawn, pull your chair to my desk." I did so rather sheepishly and with downcast eyes. "I forgive you for making up that story," she said. "I know you did it because you wanted the candy. I want you to know I appreciate your imagination," she continued, handing me a tissue to wipe my tears. A slight smile pursed my lips. "It was wrong of you to make up that story, but you have talent. I was wrong to offer a candy bar to the class for writing. I want you to love writing for writing's sake. Will you forgive me?" I threw my arms around her neck and hugged her as tightly as I could. Unbelievable! All I knew at that moment was I loved Mrs. Huggins and she loved me. She'd shown me respect and offered me grace.

Years later, when I graduated from college with my teaching degree, I wrote Mrs. Huggins to thank her for the impact she'd made on my life. Her gift of inspiration in return was a book and a six-pack of Snickers.

DAWN S. NEELY

Waves of pain reveal a pearl of joy.
CANDIS FANCHER

BROWN- AND BLUE-EYED BRIDGES

*A*fter a thirteen-hour airplane flight, a bout with boils, chicken pox, and an ear infection, our three-month-old Korean daughter Jill Joo-Mi *(Beautiful Pearl)* was placed in my arms. Curious brown eyes met tear-filled blue ones, and a global bridge was instantaneously built. Her response, amid "oohs" and "ahhs," cheers, and airport hoopla, was a calm, infectious smile. In her eyes was the bright reflection of her courageous birth mom who had surely caressed this gemlike face with her tears of sorrow, love, and hope.

Trembling with joy and anticipation, I wondered if I could meet my daughter's expectations. Could I cultivate her rich Korean heritage and blend it with her "adopted" American culture while preserving the core of her spirit? What a humbling responsibility! I wondered if both pain and promise were inherent in every adoption bundle—pain and longing for an unknown past, which may forever remain a mystery, and the promise of an unknown future.

For Jill Joo-Mi, the early years were filled with excitement and wonder. Her experiences included singing in a cross-cultural choir, proudly wearing a traditional Korean dress to show-and-tell, and entering a Minnesota restaurant in the center-stage glow of curious glances and warm smiles. Yes, home in the land of 10,000 blond-haired, blue-eyed Scandinavians was indeed a great place to be.

The novelty of the early years dimmed into the shade of pre-teen self-discovery. It began the day a classmate recited a silly verse about slanted eyes. Soon after that episode, Jill stood in the mirror frowning at her reflection.

"I don't like my dark skin!"

"Jill, I'd give a million dollars for your skin," responded Chad, her red-headed big brother who burns upon contact with the sun.

Her longing for connection to the family tree of origin intensifies on birthdays. Jill's birthday wishes have included:

"I wish that I had some of your traits in me."

"I wish that I looked like my family and friends."

"I wish that my face wasn't flat!"

I pray that someday she will fully claim her inner and outer beauty, and that she will discover peace and balance in the unfolding process. Even in the presence of birthday celebrations, Jill slips into those silent moments, desiring to bridge a void only she can fully understand. This is when we gravitate to our favorite Korean restaurant. The music of the chopsticks and calm of the Korean surroundings seem to soothe an aching heart.

Recently I asked Jill Joo-Mi, now a teenager, one of those famous *Mom* questions: "What is the disadvantage of being adopted?"

"I look different," she said without hesitation.

Probing further, I launched my second question: "Then, what is the advantage of being adopted?"

"I look *different!*" she answered confidently.

Ah . . . that's the paradox of this awesome adoption journey. Our conversation concluded with my final question: "On a scale of one to ten, how happy are you?" Holding my breath I waited.

She paused, looked at me with those amazing brown eyes, and flashed her trademark smile. "Nine and one-half," she replied.

Grinning at her, I knew that this brown-eyed, blue-eyed bridge would stand firm forever!

CANDIS FANCHER

THE TEMPERED BELL

*E*ntranced, I watched as the curtains came up on *A Chorus Line*, the first professional musical I'd seen. Music boomed and legs kicked as high as clouds, but the voice of the star character, Cassie, inspired something even more personal in me. I too wanted to dance and sing out a solo like an enchantress. To be a bell for the notes that would ring out to the audience. It was my dream, I decided without a quiver. I wanted to be like Cassie, but most of all, I wanted to be a *star*. I was ten years old.

Jumping in with both feet, I began dance lessons that year, and voice lessons soon followed. I worked hard at both, and luck stuck close to my side, providing me with one opportunity and award after another. Not only was life easy, but somehow I figured it owed me something. So, like the character of Cassie, I decided to collect. In the play, Cassie had become a quick success on Broadway and moved to Los Angeles to become a film star. But she failed and eventually went crawling back to New York to plead for a job in the chorus so she could dance again. Of course, I would change those last scenes. Only success for me.

Feeling the glee of a ten-year-old, I rushed through high school, graduated early, sold most of my stuff, and drove out to Los Angeles with my dream in hand: to dance and sing. My confidence never allowed me to have a backup plan. *Success will see me through,* I thought, as I started calling on talent agencies and restaurants. *This will be a sweet deal,* I thought, *a waitress job at night, and auditions during the day.* The beginnings of a real career.

Doors awaited, ready for me to open them. But just as they open, they can also close—with a thud. The first door, at a talent agency, told me rather summarily that they didn't want to see me unless I was a member of the union. And to do that, I had to be in a movie, or take their acting course. But my budget barely covered the cost of food, much less the money for a class.

Certainly door two would solve all that. I knew from experience that success runs a smooth course. So all I had to do was ask. But the restaurants didn't want to see me either—unless I had two years' experience in food service. My plan was off to a bad start, and the sound of doors closing was not the "bell" sound I had hoped to hear. Where was my opportunity to dance and sing?

Scared into action for the first time in my life, I grasped for a job, a job that would sustain me over this obvious hiccup. This was Plan B, not my plan at all, I thought, as I took a sales job in retail. Over the next two years, it paid the bills all right, but it left me no time to pursue my dream. My dream? Where was my dream? Finally, when my hope was all but gone, opportunity knocked. A customer in my store said he was a director, and I recognized his name.

"Well," I said, standing a little taller, "I happen to be an actor." As if I'm the only one in Los Angeles! Before I knew it, he gave me the chance to take his acting classes for free. Some of his students had received bit parts in movies. At last I had my foot in the door.

As I walked into my first class, I heard the other students, all chatting about the films they had finished and the current ones they had parts in. I was the only person in the room who had never seen a movie camera. Argh!

"Erika, I want you to go on stage and talk for five minutes." The director caught me off guard. Pushing myself out of my chair, I walked on stage, then simply froze. Staring out at these people, I couldn't say a word. My heart sank, and the last ounce of my self-esteem dwindled into nothingness as I ran out of that class—and kept running, all the way back to St. Louis.

During the time in Los Angeles, as I worked my fifty-eight hours a week, I had accomplished something, though. Along with becoming depressed, I had gained weight eating cheap, greasy food. After two years, I came back home, to the home of my success, now broke, overweight, and mentally beaten.

It took a year to regain my confidence and lose the weight. A valuable year of choices and inner changes. Then there it was, in the newspaper. Auditions for the show *A Chorus Line!* I felt fear and excitement at the same time. I was afraid I would freeze again. But I also knew Cassie's story was my story. I'm "crawling" back too, wanting to dance and sing. *This is your dream, your show of shows.* I reminded myself. The thought of just a small part gave me goose bumps. Encouraged by friends and a mom who always saw the best in me, I nervously headed for the cattle call.

Six hours later, seven of us still remained on stage, dancing and singing as we tried out for the main roles. After the audition, I ran to my car and burst into tears. I had not felt this good about myself in so many years. Just to be *considered* for my dream role was itself a dream.

One week later, the director called and asked if I would consider playing the lead part of Cassie for her production. Consider? "Yes!" I answered excitedly.

Dancing my heart out, and singing a legendary ten-minute solo with an orchestra behind me was a thrill, but there was even more to my newfound success. As I danced, I felt like Cassie at her peak. As I sang, I felt like a tempered bell, having grown stronger and richer from all my ups and downs.

The director said my portrayal of Cassie was amazingly authentic. Now I realized that all my lessons, practicing, hardships, hard work, and pain had groomed me perfectly for the part.

ERIKA EBERHARDT

THE LONG RIDE HOME

"*I* *want to look like you, Mommy, not like Daddy.*"

Mom said, "Well, you do look like me, and you look like Daddy too. Baby, God made you so special that he decided to make you look like the man I love the most—and that's your daddy."

I'll never forget the hatred I felt for my dark skin color. At the ripe age of three, I was already worrying about the social standards set by society. My mother has always set the standard of beauty in my eyes with her brown hair and light, creamy skin. I wanted her looks so much, but they were something I could never have.

At the age of four, I was still not at ease about the color of my skin. Every day my mother would pick me up from day care, scoop me up in her arms, and carry me to the car. She usually wore a long, soft skirt that brushed my face as it blew in the hot humid breeze. One day, when she came to get me she felt a tug at her skirt. It was Billy, a kid in my day care. "How come Victoria's so dark and you're so light?" Billy asked. "Are you her mommy?"

We were quiet as we drove home. As I watched Mom cry, I became very upset and began to believe that I was not her daughter. I waited for the day when she would tell me that I was adopted.

As I grew up, I thought I was growing out of my complex about my skin color. In the sixth grade, I went off to summer camp. The day my parents came to pick me up, my mom and I

did our bonding ritual—we went shopping. I had the same grubby camp clothes I'd worn all summer on as we headed off together.

We started out at a boutique we'd never been in before. It was one of those great shopping days where everything I tried on fit. Mom was excited too and said I could have them all. We went up to the cash register to pay, and the salesclerk behind the counter asked Mom, while looking down at me, "Do you want one of our attendants to take your bags, or your maid?" Furious, Mom demanded her money back, and we left. It was another long ride home. Both of us cried. I cried out of hurt. My mother cried because she did not have anything comforting to say. This time, though, I took comfort in her tears.

A year later, I tried out for cheerleader at my school. Since the first grade, when I had seen my first pep rally, I wanted to be a cheerleader. Tryouts for me came toward the end of seventh grade.

After two weeks of practicing new rigorous and physically challenging moves learned from cheerleading camp, twenty of us were as ready as we'd ever be for tryouts. The judges watched us perform, and our anxiety and anticipation were building as we waited for the results. We huddled together, holding hands, hearts pounding. As the new squad members were being called out, my heart sank with each name—until I heard, "Victoria Hurtado!" Every girl who made it had wanted the position just as badly as I did, and we all cried out of pure joy. The next day, friends and faculty showered us with flowers and little gifts to congratulate us on our accomplishment.

I never noticed the squad was predominantly white, with only two Hispanic girls, Christina and me. Not until a male student said to Christina, "The only reason you and Victoria got to be cheerleaders is that the judges needed minorities on the squad. You know—a quota." I told my mom on another long ride home. We both cried. I cried out of fear that a quota existed. My

mom cried out of fear that she could hate the boy who'd said those things.

Now in college, I don't know if I still resent the people who hurt me on my long ride here—I like to think not. But I do know that I have grown up a lot since all that pain. With each new accomplishment under my belt, I care less what other people think. I've learned that on the other side of resentment is acceptance. Today, I not only accept my honey-colored skin, I've grown to love it—and myself—just the way I am.

VICTORIA MARISSA HURTADO

It's great to be a woman today and raise your voice
and have some fun doing it.
SHANIA TWAIN

ZAPPED

t 4:45 P.M. *one beautiful day last spring, I was* skipping onto the train with all my bags full of sunscreen and tank tops. In less than seven hours, after a plane and train ride, I would be sitting on the beach in Maui with my all-time favorite cousin, Dana. *Yes!* I thought to myself. *This is really happening.*

When I came back to reality, my eyes began dancing all over the place, searching for something interesting to look at. The first thing I saw was the old woman across from me, practically steaming with frustration. Her seat was twisted around to face mine, and it wouldn't go back into position to face forward. That's when I first noticed him. A dirty-blond-haired boy with sky blue eyes crouched over trying to help the woman with her seat. He stood up.

"I can't get it," he said, "but I'll switch seats with you, if you'd like."

"Well, thank you, I think I'll do that." She looked at me sourly, as if to blame me for the stuck seat, yanked her bag from the floor, and sat down in the boy's seat. When she wasn't looking, he made a face, and I couldn't help but laugh. I felt my face going pink when we looked at each other, but so did his, so I was okay. In the awkward silence that followed, I took out a book, and he began to draw. *Oh, great,* I thought. *Is it going to be like this the whole time?* To my relief, ten minutes later he surprised me by asking my name.

"Robin," I replied. "What's yours?"

"Lucas," he replied.

We immediately launched into fun conversation. We were having the time of our lives as the train chugged along. I was amazed at how comfortable I was talking with him. To others, it probably looked as though we were old friends, even though we'd only known each other a couple of hours. As our conversation went on, I liked him more and more. He wrote the word "zapped" on my hand, which, as every seventh-grader knows, means that when you hear your name, no matter who says it, you have to say "I love you" to them. *Oh bummer,* I thought, sarcastically. He kept ending every sentence with "Robin," so the words "I love you" kept rolling out of my mouth.

Before we knew it, the train started slowing and screeched to a halt. We got off the train and slowly said our last "I love you's" and then went our separate ways. All I knew was his first name, and this thought didn't hit me until he disappeared into the station.

"There you are!" my cousin Dana said. I shook myself out of my love-stricken daze and gave her a hug.

My entire trip to Maui was overshadowed with images of Lucas, plans to bribe someone at the train station into telling me his phone number, and being mad at myself for not getting his last name and number in the first place. I thought about him so much that it was pathetic. I never even noticed all the cute guys in Maui! And I continued to think about him all summer long.

Now, with a new school year just starting, I'm definitely older and wiser. I can't believe I wasted all that time thinking about a boy on a train. I mean he was great and all, but *so what?* Life is just too short. And, as every *eighth*-grader knows, there are plenty of fish in the sea.

ROBIN RICHARDS

CAMP GRAMMA

I *am my grandmother's child, raised by her from* babyhood, when my parents were busy sorting out their own lives, too young themselves to have two children. A generation missing between us, Gramma patched the rift together seamlessly with her constant love and creative attention.

We were lucky, my brother and I, because we grew up with magic Gramma-made adventures. From the time I was little, I handled pocketknives, hammers, hatchets, and saws. I learned to catch fish with a long stick and a piece of fishing line, tied with a hook and baited with a squiggly worm from under a rock. I learned to build fires and bake bread in an outdoor oven. I learned to sew and to knit. I learned to swing across the creek on our Tarzan ropes and make friends of squirrels and snakes. I remember mud pies, a genuine yellow playhouse, and backyard wienie roasts. I learned to read books in a silent meadow of wildflowers, the wind and the sun my company. I loved and felt loved.

The year, the month, the precise day that it began, I cannot say. I may even have lost some years when everyone else began to grow up, and I stayed living in my imagination in my childhood in my Gramma's world.

Then I was thrown, suddenly and sharply, into a disenchanted life. My father came one day to claim me, having remarried and set up house in another city, a big city, 500 miles away. I said goodbye to my beloved grandparents and went with my suitcase and my brother to my father's new family.

I knew how to sew and knit and fish and hike. But I had absolutely no idea of how to apply makeup, shave my legs, or blow-dry my hair. I was skinny. I didn't know how to play sports or the flute. I couldn't sing, or dance ballet. My ears weren't pierced (until Suzette Gerz got a hold of me with two ice cubes and a needle during a sleep over).

To make things worse, I had an evil stepmother, which was a grave disappointment because I was so happy to finally have a mom. And this woman had her own daughter, my horrid stepsister, who was older and bigger than me, mean, and always right. About the time this new sister dropped me on my head and fractured my collarbone, my dad's marriage was in trouble.

Our struggling picture-perfect new family imploded, scattering shrapnel into the flesh of all our best intentions. Father divorced and tried with hopeless sincerity to raise two adolescents by himself before he sent me back with my suitcase and my brother to my gramma. To my home.

But it was too late. I had become a teenager. Suddenly, high school was happening, and I was unprepared. It didn't take long in this self-regulating culture to learn *the rules*. All the rules centered around the great striving to be popular. And everybody knew who was and who was not. You couldn't fake it. If you weren't in the "in" crowd, the best you could hope for was to be the most in of the "out" crowd. And the out crowd was made up of the masses, a disordered conglomeration of numerous little pods of the common and the ordinary. The in crowd had order and prosperity. Members of the out crowd were divided and conquered from the start.

Then there was the great conspiracy that we all just accepted. The teachers and coaches and counselors were all in on it. In on the great popularity plot, keeping the chosen few at the top. How else did only the popular girls ever get to be the cheerleaders? And the basketball stars: how was it that the popular kids were also the most talented among us?

It was a rule—an unwritten social code of our time. Pretty girls had straight hair. Unless you permed it. Permed, curly hair was okay. If you had naturally curly hair, like I had, you were automatically an out-crowder. Naturally curly hair—particularly if it was brown—was not only *out,* it was a genetic hint that a person was less, inferior, made of flawed material.

To be a popular girl, you couldn't be more that five feet five inches tall either. Another unwritten, unspoken rule. Tall girls, like me, loomed gangly and awkward over the rest, hunching our shoulders to look shorter, shifting our big feet, and dangling our hands nervously around our knees.

So I circulated on the fringes, trying to become the most in of my little out-pod, and president of the Future Homemakers of America. An accomplishment that embarrasses me to this day.

It was useless to know how to hook a worm on a fishing line when everyone else was concerned with the really important matters. Matters of clothes and hair and makeup—and of flirting. I was a spaz in my imagination, in my memory, of that time. I clowned my way through this space of life, knowing that if I ever stopped laughing, the tears would come.

So much changed. I was afraid of snakes. I looked like a goon in a swimsuit. I read alone in my room, a lot. I pouted and complained when I didn't get my way. I got lectured, a lot. I felt as though my grandparents were space aliens, put here to make my life difficult.

The rift of that missing generation suddenly split wide open, vast and immeasurably deep. But I was raised to be good and to mind, and I did. I got good grades and minded my teachers. I had good friends and minded the rules. By the time I graduated, I had a bona fide boyfriend, a plan for college, and a map for happiness. I was growing up, but I was bent on rebelling, and I swore that I would never, ever be like my grandmother. I would wrestle through the years to keep that promise to myself, and I would fail, time after time.

My body has long since grown into itself, and my free-flowing, naturally curly hair is back in style. Although I never learned to dance or play the flute, and my map for happiness has changed many times, I've created my own style of living in the world. I've turned the scars of youth into badges of grace.

What matters to me most, though, is something altogether different. It is that I have a great appreciation for the natural world and a tremendous compassion for all life on earth. I can sew and knit and fish and camp because, once upon a treasured time, I had someone teach me. I had a Gramma who taught me through her devoted attention, every day, to love and be loved. And to keep a secret sanctuary—a place of delight—in the wild woods of my heart.

KYLA MERWIN

IV

VISION KEEPERS

*Learn to get in touch with the silence within yourself and know
that everything in this life has a purpose.*

ELISABETH KÜBLER-ROSS

LIFE-SCHOOL TIPS I'D TELL MY DAUGHTER

1. Young women your age who look older than you also look older than you years later when they don't want to!
2. You don't need to chase guys, let them chase you. They are wired for it.
3. Women who use their brains get ahead. You don't need to play dumb for anyone.
4. If you don't love yourself on the inside, it's hard for others to love you on the outside.
5. Young women who stay with guys who treat them poorly don't think they deserve any better.
6. The higher your self-esteem, the healthier the people will be that you attract.
7. Once you've given away your virginity, you can never have it back.
8. The truth is always easier than a lie—you never have to remember what you said.
9. It's okay to say no to something when no one else does. You will be respected for it later.
10. If you stay away from other cars when you drive, you'll live longer.
11. If you ride a motorcycle without a helmet, you've got a screw loose!
12. Think ahead about what you'd say yes to and no to. When that kind of decision comes your way, you'll already know what to do.
13. You can learn a lot about a guy by meeting his parents.

14. Date rape is never your fault. Report it.
15. Invite God in to help you with your problems. Give him something to do.
16. Watch at least one wholesome, funny show a week. Laughing produces feel-good endorphins in your body that help ward off disease. And laughing keeps you optimistic.
17. Get lost in a great book—it's therapeutic.
18. If someone treats you rudely, chances are they are having a bad day. Be compassionate back.
19. What goes around comes around—good and bad.
20. Being a "late bloomer" can be a good thing—you can learn from everyone else's mistakes.
21. Be grateful for something each day.
22. Don't believe what your school counselor has to say about your future if you know you can do better.
23. If you say, "I had no choice," you're kidding yourself.
24. Don't ever assume that life will be fair. Life just is.
25. Great kissers have had a lot of practice—with someone else.
26. If you spend time with people who do bad things—on some level you agree with what they're doing.
27. Compliment someone each day.
28. You don't appreciate anything fully unless you've earned it.
29. Skinny, undernourished bodies are out. Strong, healthy bodies are in.
30. Trust your intuition. Women have been given an abundant supply of it for a reason.
31. Love yourself deeply—there is no one else just like you!

KAY ALLENBAUGH

To miss the opportunities of the "wild" because we judge them bad,
intolerable or dangerous may require missing the glory
of the journey & the opportunities that result.
MARY ELLEN BRANDEBURG

WEAVING A TAPESTRY
OF LIFE

*I*didn't know how I would get there, but I knew I
wanted to go to Europe someday. Early on, my German-
speaking friends, Antje and Kirstin, pulled me into their tapestry of hard sounds and earthy melodies in our childhood
games. That tug of sounds stayed with me long after the games
were outgrown when I moved into a post–high school job as a
receptionist. Many of the firm's secretaries had started, as I had,
out of high school with dreams of their own, but their faces told
of dreams worn away by years of being overworked, disappointed, and burned out.

I always thought I was finished with school, but I decided to
put myself through college, more as a way to escape my humdrum job than anything else. To my surprise, I discovered I loved
to learn. I found the university atmosphere intoxicating; it
stretched my mind and challenged me. Being involved and learning as much as possible became my aim and a way to support my
dream of European travel and exploration.

On quiet Sundays, I made my way through piles of magazines

to create a gigantic six-by-four-foot collage. Baroque gardens, Gothic cathedrals, cobblestone streets, windmills, Roman ruins, brick row houses, ancient temples, historic museums, and outdoor cafés covered one of my dorm walls at college.

In my senior year, after I had been dreaming of Europe for years with intangible results, my German professor approached me with the name of an Austrian family who needed a nanny. The following week, I met with the family's stateside representative and that afternoon applied for my passport. As with my first few steps on campus, I felt a deep *yes*. I could feel the threads of my childhood tapestry coming together in my fingers.

The following August, I boarded the plane for Vienna, despite all my fears and doubts.

"You're not coming back," a girlfriend of mine said. "You'll meet a prince and live happily ever after."

"No, no," I replied, "I'll be back in a year to start on my master's degree."

The first day I found myself alone in the family's home in Vienna, I had no idea what was ahead of me. The couple went off to work. I gathered all my courage to fight off the "what ifs" about my shaky German and walked around the block. I discovered Beethoven's and Schubert's first resting place just around the corner from where I lived. My courage and circles enlarged until I found myself exploring the entire city by tram and underground.

My foremost daily challenge, besides communicating in German, was the couple's two-year-old. Nearing the end of our first six months together, my charge and I were set with the goal of potty training. On one particular day, we had an unsuccessful lesson, and in my attempt to clean up little Mara, I managed to get dirty. The doorbell rang. It rang again. Once more. And again. This kept up until I yelled in German, "Just a moment!" I ran to change my sweatshirt and opened the door. I caught myself saying, "Come in," without knowing who the man was because in that moment, I *knew* I would marry him.

David turned out to be a neighbor from the first floor wanting to use the phone because his wasn't working. We'd been living in the same house, shopping in the same shops, and running in the same park for the last six months without ever seeing each other. Since all the phones in the district weren't working, David stayed and chatted. The next day he returned because he "had to talk to the couple about some house matters." He invited me over for coffee to test out his new espresso machine. I skipped my German lesson and choked down espresso while I studied David's dark red lips and crooked smile over the rim of my demitasse cup. We talked for hours.

After I completed my year as nanny, David suggested I stay and work on my master's at the University of Vienna. When I saw the old university building and its reading room, with long wooden tables and green lamps, I felt another *yes*. Convincing me to stay wasn't difficult. Austria has no major drug problem, and it has schools without weapons, affordable higher education, socialized medicine, few homeless, stringent recycling, no atomic energy, gourmet cuisine, and endless concerts, operas, galleries, balls, and exhibits. Yes, yes, yes. I made a tight fist around that thread in my hand. All of those yeses brought me to another *yes*—the legal one with David nearly five years later.

Sometimes I marvel at how those dreamy hard sounds and earthy melodies of childhood are my gift to weave daily. What was once a six-by-four-foot collage on my dorm wall has become my living, breathing tapestry. My life is far better than any I could have imagined. It's not without a few bumps and jolts and a bit of chaos, but I say *yes* to the chaos the same way I say *yes* to the rest of it because the glory of something handmade is in the making.

KRISTA VEENKER ROTHSCHILD

I cannot be defined by what other people think.
OPRAH WINFREY

DEFINING YOURSELF

I thought my career was over, and it hadn't started yet. Dressed in a Casual Corner suit, I was sitting in a downtown Pittsburgh parking lot, sobbing into a Burger King napkin. Would I ever make it, or would I be gobbled up like a cheeseburger?

I had just come out of a media career day. As a twenty-one-year-old journalism major graduating from Duquesne University, I was eager to find a job and prove I was somebody. I hoped someone at the job fair would hire me.

After all, I was a driven student who had done all the "right" things. I had held internships with a television station and a PR firm, had had a 3.76 GPA, and I was active in a Women in Communications group.

I was even serious with my writing as a kid. In fifth grade, I created a neighborhood newspaper that I sold to everyone on my street. I hired my brother as the sportswriter—and later fired him because he would rather play ball than write about it. And I hired a girlfriend as my secretary. I fired her too, because she couldn't type. In high school, I reported for the school television station.

At a media career day, I talked with several news outlets, gave out my résumé, and showed them my portfolio. They had no positions available but kindly offered advice in breaking into that competitive field. I was disappointed, but I decided to make one last stop to talk with a media representative who was sitting alone.

I'll see what he has to say, I thought. *You never know when you might find the coveted first journalism job. The one that screams, "I've made it! I've broken in!"*

I approached the man timidly. His arms were folded in front of him as if he didn't want to be there. I introduced myself with a firm handshake. His grip was dead weight. I was now the next victim.

"Well, what's your story?" he asked.

Story? Okay, he's testing me. He wants a headline of my life, a sound bite of my world. I rattled off my grade point average, work ethic, and everything else my college advisers told me to say when job hunting. Silence. *Yikes,* I thought, *maybe he wanted to hear about my activities instead?*

"Ms. Mildren," he said.

"Uh, it's Meldrum."

"Whatever," he snapped. "Listen, you're not qualified to be a reporter here."

I sat there stunned. It felt as if I were his midday snack.

"In fact," he continued, "I don't think you're even qualified to be sitting here talking with me."

The look on my face must have said, "Keep it coming. I enjoy being bashed in the head. It reminds me of a good root canal."

"At my organization, we don't want to even *talk* to you unless you have five to ten years' experience. You're just taking up my time."

I felt a lump in my throat. "Well, I've had, uh, internships and . . ."

"Means nothing. It's real experience we want. You don't have it. You couldn't do this job, and we don't want you."

Everything I worked for *means nothing*? I turned and dashed outside, feeling the tears slide down my hot cheeks. I didn't have the *right* to be in his booth? I was a nobody. Would anybody let me be somebody?

A career-day sponsor told me later that they wouldn't be inviting him back again. I wish I could say I felt better. After I graduated, I spent the next three months looking for work, and I beat myself up in the process—dwelling on all the negative remarks I'd heard. My dentist even had input. "You'll never make it in television with those teeth," he'd said. Maybe I wasn't good-looking enough for television, or a good enough writer for newspapers.

But soon I found a position in a national press office for a federal agency in Washington, D.C. I started at the bottom and relentlessly worked my way up. Within five years, I was speech writing for the director and other officials, setting up press conferences, doing live radio interviews, and writing and editing a publication. In the evenings, I toiled as an anchor and reporter for a cable television station.

The world didn't greet me with open arms when I graduated, but I learned to stop letting others define me. I began defining myself. I wasn't my job. My sense of self-worth didn't descend on me the day someone decided I was "good enough" for a job. Confidence is an evolution. In my case, it came from moving—alone—400 miles from my family. From dealing with a live mouse stuck in a glue trap in my bathroom. From managing to go to work the day after my boyfriend said he didn't love me anymore. From being stuck in the rain on the Pennsylvania Turnpike when my windshield wipers blew off—and engineering a twisty tie to put them back on. Confidence came from looking at myself in the mirror, years later, knowing I'd won.

And Mr. "Means Nothing"? He called my office one day needing information. I didn't tell him who I was, and I put him on hold for several minutes.

"Thanks for waiting," I said when I came back to him. "*Newsweek* and the *Washington Post* were ahead of you. We rank calls in order of importance."

KRISTINE MELDRUM DENHOLM

Enough is as good as a feast.
KATHARINE TYNAN

CHARACTER STUDY

*I*t pays to be an artist. At least that's what I thought when as a freshman in high school, I signed up for my favorite class. Instead of math or science, ahh, to take an elective—to be in the art class, with other artists, with drawing paper and drawing tools. And . . . with assignments. Oh no!

I hadn't thought that far ahead! What was I thinking? I was no artist. And I knew it when we all took charcoal in hand, and followed Mr. Matoush's direction to close our eyes! How could we draw like this? But Mr. Matoush knew what he was doing, thank goodness. By using this technique called contour drawing, we came to find the spirit of a thing. As we opened and closed our eyes, we loosened up and actually felt closer to what we drew. Even if the drawing looked cockeyed or messy, it had more character than our careful attempts at perfection.

This helped my performance anxieties somewhat, but as I entered class the next day, my worries of "not enoughness" resurfaced. "Now what?" I thought miserably, as I knew I'd have to use my smooth charcoal and fresh drawing paper to actually make a true representation of something. Would it even come close to what I saw? More to the point, would it look dumb?

Would I need to run and hide my head from the "real" artists in the class?

Through my insecurities, I watched Mr. Matoush's black mustache move. On one level, I knew he spoke about an important assignment. On another level, I simply didn't want to hear it. I felt more and more like a freshman.

"Draw a person," Matoush said simply. I waited for more. Maybe an explanation. But that was it.

Ha! I can do that, one part of me said.

Ha! Are you kidding? another part of me retorted—more loudly. I carried this conflicting conversation around with me all week. After all, I had time. The inspiration would come. *Tomorrow would be a good day,* I thought. Trouble was, I thought it again and again, until it was too late.

Tonight's the night, I decided, cornered. But who will I draw? Not only who is around—but who will sit still? And why draw someone real, I figured, when the drawing wouldn't look like them anyway. How embarrassing!

So-o-o, with real creativity, I pulled out my trusty *Seventeen* magazine. Perfect, I thought, there's plenty of beauty here! With drawing charcoal in hand, I bent to my task—working, working, oblivious to all other things.

A fence rail emerged, then a good-looking model perched upon it. A model? My artist's eyes looked, and looked again. This wasn't a real person. This was a model! Before me on the paper, an empty shell stared back. Startled, I felt concepts fly around me.

But I thought this was what it was about. Looking beautiful. Everything just right. The right clothes. The right hairstyle. The ...

My concept of beauty fell like crystal shards at my feet.

I stopped and put my charcoal down. Is this what we are aiming at—all of us women and soon to be women? Is this empty beauty "enough"?

Before the night ended, I knew I was "enough" in a different way. The next day I went to see the master. Confessing my plight, I begged for another week.

"Will you do twice as much?" Matoush sparred, a kindly twinkle in his eyes. I liked that twinkle but wondered, *Where did that spark of life come from? How did he get it?*

"Yes," I replied gratefully. And then I settled in to art class—knowing I was enough. Knowing all of us are enough. And I set out to draw old people with lines, or young people laughing, or real people pondering life's moments. No more models perched all too perfectly on fences. Picking up my charcoal with a new-found zeal, I set out to do a character study.

These were the years before we knew the words *anorexia* or *bulimia*. But as teenage girls, we did know the stress of images, all too glossy, all too perfect. But not all of us had the opportunity to enter an art class and see what beauty really was—and wasn't.

That experience changed the way I looked at life and the way I valued the character in each person. I wonder if Mr. Matoush knew everything he taught us. Somehow, I think he did.

Charcoal in hand, I found I was right: it pays to be an artist. And the next week, carrying new drawings under my arm, I walked in to see Mr. Matoush. "Very good," he said, smiling at the new twinkle in my eye. And I smiled back, knowing the twinkle was very much like his.

SHEILA STEPHENS

FIRST IMPRESSIONS

*T*he summer before seventh grade, I spent a lot of time glancing into mirrors. I decided that developing and maintaining the right smile would camouflage my total fear about junior high.

School district policy yanked all of us from the security of neighborhood buildings and thrust us into the large junior high complex way across town. Friends who had played kick the can in the street and volleyball in backyards and had grown up closely together were now going to be scattered into different "sections," marched down long hallways, and placed at the mercy of several teachers daily.

This meant no more skipping home for lunch, waving to neighbors, and enjoying the singing of birds. Instead, my folks would be driving me to school daily, and I'd be introduced to such mysterious things as hamburger gravy in a basement cafeteria accompanied by major noise pollution.

The inevitable first day arrived. I was one in a crowd of swarming boys and girls converging from all directions to begin a new era. Opening the car door, I tried my new smile out on my mom, then frantically searched for my "homeroom."

The room was about half full when I arrived, and I slipped into my assigned alphabetical seat. Afraid to make eye contact with anyone, I stared ahead and held my breath. Etched in my memory is the moment my smile collapsed and my confidence level ebbed below baseline. In walked (strutted, actually) a cool girl dressed as if she'd just walked off the set of *90210*. In that instant, my brand-new clothes felt ridiculously simple, and the distance from elementary school to this new world seemed to span a universe.

She had the attention of the entire group, certainly the boys! No way would I ever be able to handle class with this flirt, let alone ever approach someone like her. It was going to be a long year, worse when I soon discovered she and I shared the same first name: Linda.

I convinced myself that she must be wearing a padded bra—nobody's that perfect. A tap on my shoulder interrupted my growing apprehensions, and I welcomed a reason to turn around.

"Hi! I'm Nancy."

Nancy's smile lit up her entire face. Without exchanging words, we had a mutual understanding about what we had just witnessed. Fortunately, all our teachers alphabetized their seating charts, so Nancy sat behind me in every class that day. Her smile reflected back to me better than any mirror. She joined me in the cafeteria chaos, making it more tolerable.

We quickly learned during those lunch periods that the stuff we ate didn't matter nearly as much as the stuff we talked about. As our circle grew from that first day and over the next six years, we all learned volumes about inequalities and inner qualities. We discovered how much more alike we were than different, as we shared our insecurities and the ups and downs that come with being that age.

Linda's enthusiasm made her a role model for many in our class, and it finally dawned on me that she was self-assured and at the same time just one of us. Nancy and I were amazed with Linda's ability to talk to boys and even more impressed with how quickly she brought us into those conversations. Lunchtime *really* got more interesting once the boys started sitting at our table. By watching Linda, I began to understand what it means to be comfortable with just being yourself.

I knew way back then that first impressions can indeed be lasting ones, and that Nancy and I would remain good friends. What I didn't know is what I might have missed if I hadn't been open to changing my initial negative impressions of Linda.

Nearly four decades later, Nancy, Linda, and I often talk about our early first impressions, and our lasting ones, laughing and giggling exactly as we did all those years ago. Linda and I eventually stood up for each other at our weddings, which seems a long distance to travel from that first day we walked separately into seventh-grade homeroom.

LINDA G. ENGEL

Soul food is our personal passport to the past.
SARAH BAN BREATHNACH

IN THE COMPANY OF WOMEN

*E*very summer my grandmother planted a garden. Not just a six-by-six square plot of earth in her backyard, but a vast, expansive, sacred place, guarded by a fence and a gate. This garden was her pride and joy, and for me, as a child, a frightening mystery. My grandmother ruled the passage into the garden with an iron fist. Once you were old enough to know how to walk in the rows between the plants and not on them, you were permitted entrance to pull weeds, and then only supervised and for small amounts of time. Frankly, it was not a privilege I yearned for, or relished once it was granted.

That is not to say that I didn't relish sharing in the rewards that came from my grandmother's hard work. The harvests from her garden were truly something to behold—bushels of snap beans, sweet crookneck yellow squash, and tiny red potatoes that were her personal favorite.

My grandmother sent each of her children home with bags full of these fresh vegetables whenever they came to visit, since there was no way she and my grandfather could have eaten all that the garden offered. Even better, summertime at her house meant dinners of nothing but these fresh, delicious vegetables straight from her garden. The most luscious gifts from the garden were the plump, juicy tomatoes that my brothers and I loved to eat straight off the vine while they were still warm. They were so addictive, in fact, that we bore the wrath of Grandma more than once when she caught us climbing over the fence with the prize in hand. The ends always justified the means, however, especially if one of us remembered to put the salt shaker in our pockets before starting our mission. Grandma grew tomatoes like no one else. Tomatoes that tasted unlike any I have ever had since, and in such quantity that there was nothing else to do but, come July, clean out the mason jars and can them.

The experience of canning tomatoes can be summed up easily. In a word—hot. In two words—really messy. The process involves lots of boiling water, lots of tomatoes and tomato peels, pressure cookers, and sweat. In Virginia, one usually cans tomatoes in late July or early August, just as the crop starts to wane. I had watched my mother and grandmother can tomatoes for years, and I was relieved to escape that steamy job to go out and run through the sprinkler in the backyard instead, trying to make the best of the awful summer heat and humidity. When the year finally arrived that I was recruited to help, I was less than honored.

I begrudgingly took my post at the peeling station. Surrounded by what seemed like mountains of tomatoes, I sat in silence and mourned the loss of my youthful freedom (heady thoughts for a gangly eleven-year-old). Grandma appointed each of us to our spot with exacting precision. My mom stood by the sink washing jars. Grandma poured boiling water into buckets to blanch the tomatoes in order to make peeling them easier. I sat with a dull knife and juice dripping down my arm and onto my foot, peeling and peeling, one after the other, thinking that we would never, ever be finished.

As the hours passed, a magical thing started to happen. My grandmother started to tell stories about canning tomatoes when she was a little girl on the farm in North Carolina and how this crop didn't hold a candle to those she and her sisters put up every summer. Mom told stories about her dad's adventures of trying to make the perfect bread-and-butter pickle, only to fail year after year. My grandmother filled the jars, my mom screwed on the lids, and we fell into an easy rhythm that made the hours pass quickly. I just sat silently and listened. Peeling and listening, and feeling, for the first time in my young life, a part of that secret society of women in my family who make the kitchen the heart of the home.

CARRIE D. THORNTON

CLEARING THE CLOUDS
UPON MY HEART

"*H*ow would you like to teach a seminar for our new sorority members?" the college adviser said, a meaningful but hopeful look in her eyes. "We need a leader like you to tell young women about the dangers of date rape."

"Count me in," I answered, committed to tackling new challenges, especially one that could prevent some unnecessary sorrows for the young women just coming to campus.

Two years after that class, I numbly read my own police report to my mother. My outgoing, tackle-anything nature had disappeared, and now my voice sounded hollow and flat as I read about *my rape*.

From my own experience teaching that session, I knew I needed to talk about what had happened: the surprise attack after several dates with a gorgeous student from another country. Looking back, I can see beyond my initial excitement about him. Now I can see the all-too-yellow flags. How he was *too* intriguing, *too* aggressive early on, pressing me about all kinds of things. Most relationships I'd had before started out more clumsy than that. More real, maybe.

But this was all too real. Real, yet without enough evidence to bring about a legal closure. I kept thinking about that word "enough." And life became cloudy. Not the white puffy clouds like skip across a summer sky, but the kind of ominous gray clouds that you know are here to stay, painting everything around them a paler tone. Even though I tried to focus on what I'd learned—and taught others—I still felt myself crumble, until all too soon I couldn't recognize my former self within those clouds.

So now I faced reality by hiding. And as I hid, I asked myself, *How did you let that happen?* No one knew I kept asking myself this. I darted quickly from place to place, wearing sunglasses like blinders, and baggy clothes to chase away any more attention from all-too-smooth guys.

I could do this, I thought. *I could get by.*

And I did. So this was progress, my mind told me. And a year later, still in an unacknowledged emotional coma, I finally resumed dating. At that point, I didn't realize how common it is for a victim of sexual abuse to go through a period of promiscuity and to start drinking or taking drugs. I didn't think of these activities as symptoms of my abuse. In my mind, being sexually active translated to "intimacy," and alcohol would help me cope—and help me heal. After all, I could talk about my experience when I drank, and I felt close to the men I told about my rape, so I slept with them. This, I thought, was the healing process. It would make everything better.

So why did I still hurt?

In my previous life, before the rape, I had sought new vistas and ways I could grow as a person. But now I practiced repetition. For seven years. For seven long years of countless hangovers and a bout of depression. People had tried to help, but the circle of abuse continued—now the circle of abuse at my very own hands.

All this time, my dad had been supportive of me, even inviting me over for dinner and talk. One evening the clouds parted for a minute, and I felt ready to hear something beyond my ongoing agony. As we ate, the conversation turned to something I hadn't given much thought to before. We spoke of spirituality, and even forgiveness.

I've forgiven everyone, I thought honestly. *I've forgiven my violator, the men that reminded me of him, the police, and everyone who wasn't there for me.*

And as if Dad knew what I was thinking, he quietly said, "You know, nothing will work for you until you forgive yourself."

Tears filled his eyes and mine. I left his home that night not knowing if I could take that step. I needed help from above. When I arrived home, I got down on my knees and prayed that I could forgive myself. Logically, I knew I'd done nothing wrong, but I still blamed myself.

The months that followed were some of the toughest of my life, because the anger and judgment I'd heaped on myself for so long kept my heart not only clouded over but closed. I'd lived through seven years of blaming myself, of hating myself, and to think of leaving it behind felt like giving up an addiction, a constant companion. Now I was asking to be held in the palm of God's hand.

My head kept fighting with my heart. The head that wanted to control life to protect me and help me hide. But I suddenly asked myself why I wanted to hide? And what was it I really wanted to be? And I found I no longer wanted to be the version of life that all-too-smooth student had foisted on me. So that night, I wept for all I had done to myself, and just as I had forgiven his behavior before, I finally forgave myself. And I started listening to my heart.

My heart had its own version of what it wanted my life to be. And so I walked into unknown territory, not thankful that something so bad had happened to me but realizing that in each hardship was an opportunity to grow. Now I had grown into the gentle skies of forgiveness, ones that warm you and give you strength, even on stormy days.

Today I surround my precious body and soul with loving thoughts, caring friends and family. I am thankful for a new spiritual life that makes me feel each day is to be lived meaningfully

and joyously, not just endured. Today I draw on different clothes—bright leotards and sweats—and ride my bike twenty miles to work and back. And now I have a romantic relationship based not only on caring but on mutual respect as well.

Head or heart? How would I teach that class today? I think I'd say, take some of both, but don't forget your own heart. Let it lead you to say the things held so tightly that you might break. Let it lead you also to self-forgiveness and self-love—and a whole new way of being strong.

And thinking about this gentler path that I have found, I realize the last seven years haven't been for naught. Climbing on-board my bike, I feel the strength flow through my body, and my mind, *and* my spirit. As I put sunglasses on, a smile emerges from my lips. My trusty sunglasses—today I use them not to hide, but only to help me see the way.

SHERI TERJESON

TRUE HEART

*S*hanghai, China, was in the throes of a searing August heat wave that reduced most of the refugee population to melting, dripping bundles of humanity. The annual stifling, sticky "Tiger Heat" had its choke hold on the overcrowded, restless city on the Whangpoo River.

The year was 1944. The war in Europe was still raging, although new hope for an end in sight had blossomed with the invasion of Normandy by the Allied forces. Other highlights in our lives were the lively rumors that were flying around in our Japanese detention camp that the tide had turned against the Nippon forces. Several of our friends with access to a secret shortwave radio brought us news almost daily of the heavy losses the Japanese forces were experiencing on land and sea in the Pacific.

About 18,000 Middle European Jews, who had found an uneasy sanctuary in Shanghai for a while, had been interned by the Japanese occupation army shortly after Pearl Harbor. In our fourth year of confinement, our existence had become quite unbearable from the lack of food and medicine and the deplorable sanitary conditions. A self-appointed "King of the Jews," the arrogant and psychopathic camp commander, the not-so-honorable Goya-san, with his crazy antics, contributed heavily to the constant irritations of our confinement. Life was difficult for young and old alike.

Those of us who were teenagers had no place to go, no place to play, no place to be young and carefree. We wondered what kids our age were doing in America. What did they do for leisure? What did they do for fun? What did they eat, and did they go to the movies?

My best friend, Eva Kuenstler, and I would sit for hours in the tiny courtyard of her parents' one-room dwelling, swatting at flies and mosquitoes, and speculate on what young people were doing on other continents. We wondered what they wore. What was in? There we were in our faded, old, homemade and remade dresses or skirts and blouses. We still had some things from before our exile, but they were unfit for wearing in the subtropical climate of Shanghai and had already turned gray with mildew.

Seventeen-year-old Eva was a slim, petite brunette whose thick light-brown hair with its golden highlights framed a piquant face with a full mouth and curious amber eyes. Her parents, who had been successful spice merchants in Austria, were self-involved and removed from the Oriental world they abhorred. They also had no idea what to do with a child. Until emigration, Eva had been raised by nannies and usually was given what she wanted. For quite some time now, she had quarreled bitterly with her lot, often. I got tired of her constant complaining and quoted my father's words of wisdom to her that went something like this: "Since we don't have anything better, then this must be the best." In other words, make do with reality. But words, wise or otherwise, were not what she wanted. Eva wanted "things."

Just recently, she had been keeping company with a young Hungarian girl, Elena, who had acquired a Japanese "benefactor" and enjoyed the fruits of her ill-chosen relationship. The young officer had access to a warehouse of things we had long forgotten existed. He brought her Swiss shoes, American canned goods, coffee, yards of fine silks and cotton fabrics accompanied by a handy tailor, American cigarettes, jewelry, and books. The seventeen-year-old Elena was a well-fed fashion plate, and whenever we'd meet up with her, she purred like the cat who'd swallowed the canary.

Elena was not the only young woman who bartered her self-worth for things of no worth. Quite a few European girls and married women chose to improve their lifestyle by becoming "companions" to Japanese officers and businessmen. A bunch of kids were not necessarily dispensing finger-pointing moral judgments, but simply understood that the cost of a new dress, a pair of shoes, or a meal at a restaurant came high.

One hot, sticky August afternoon, Eva announced to me in a hushed voice, ringing with excitement, that she had had it!

"I'm tired of my life," she said. "I'm sick and tired of sitting around talking about grandiose ideas and shiny ideals when I'm hungry, sweaty, and dressed in rags. I'm young, and I want to have some fun. I want clothes. I want to go to a restaurant. I want the feel of a silk dress against my skin. I want a good perfume. I want to be admired by a man, I want . . . I want . . . I want."

She swore me to secrecy as she confided that Elena was introducing her to a Japanese officer that evening who was looking for a companion. He was far away from home (weren't we all?) and lonely.

"You want to become a prostitute?" I was shocked but not surprised. "You want to sell your body (how dramatic!) for a few meals and some clothes?" I kept after her. We'd never even held hands with a boy yet and were clueless about what to expect from an intimate relationship. We'd heard some bone-chilling tales about the things some men do, however.

"Remember what we talked about at the Landerhoffs' the other night?" I nagged.

Eva looked away.

The Landerhoffs were a wonderful couple who invited young

people into their tiny quarters to eat peanuts, drink lukewarm tea, and discuss anything from the life cycle of the butterfly, to Lao-tse, Greek philosophers, Voltaire, and the Russian Revolution. Our hosts challenged our intellect, fed our minds to overflow, taught us the power of visions, and gave us the opportunity to learn to think beyond our pitiful existence.

"When you meet that man tonight," I said, breaking into Eva's mood, "just remember our discussion. We all agreed that we defined our lives by the way we met challenges and how we handled the hard knocks. Mr. Landerhoff also made us understand that for every action there was a consequence. He reminded us that good times don't make us strong, bad times do."

"Well"—Eva got to her feet—"I've had all I want of bad times, and furthermore," she added, tossing her magnificent head of hair for emphasis, "I don't need approval from you or anybody else. My heart tells me what to do."

"Good," I yelled after her, "just be sure to check in with your heart one more time before . . ."

The Tiger Heat lost its momentum, the air cooled down enough to bring some relief, moods improved, and life seemed easier. I didn't see Eva for several days but finally gave in to my inner nagging and went to her house. She opened the door wearing the same old cotton skirt and faded shirt knotted at the waist. *Well,* I thought to myself, *the handy tailor must not have caught up with her yet.* She smiled at me a bit sheepishly and, without saying a word, led the way through the family's room to our perch in the courtyard.

"Well," I said, challenging her silence. "What happened?"

She hid her face in her hands, dropped them again, sober amber eyes looking straight at me, and said with a sigh, "Nothing. Nothing happened. I changed my mind. I never went to meet that man. My act of bravado and daring was just that—an act. I thought about it a lot more after you left. I decided that leading that kind of a life was one memory I didn't want to have. You were right, I really wasn't following my heart at all. I hadn't even asked. When I finally did ask my heart, I was given the right answer. The heart never lies."

URSULA BACON

V

OVER, UNDER, OR THROUGH

We like to pretend it is hard to follow our heart's dreams.
The truth is, it is difficult to avoid walking through
the many doors that will open.

JULIA CAMERON

ON MY OWN

*A*s *I entered college, I had a plan. I would learn* everything I could possibly pack into my brain over the next four years, I would meet a lot of interesting people, and I would live in London at some point after graduation. The last thing on my mind was finding a husband; there were so many other things on my mind! Besides, I didn't particularly want to get married anyway.

Over the next three years, I stayed on course. I double-majored in history and English, I read what seemed like a million books, and I became involved in several campus organizations. But what I enjoyed the most were the endless afternoons spent sipping tea with my women friends, sharing our views on every subject from the latest political scandal to the best books of the century. We laughed and cried through our achievements, and we always supported one another through our setbacks.

Strangely, in the fall of my senior year, there seemed to be a recurring topic in our conversations. It unsettled me to see my witty and wonderful friends become so fixated on the idea of getting engaged before graduation. It was as if life began with a proposal and a diamond ring. "After all," my friend Ellen said, "college is the only time in our lives that we will be surrounded by so many men our age. If it doesn't happen now, the odds of meeting Mr. Right decrease so dramatically I don't even want to think about it!"

I was completely lost. I didn't understand what was happening to the women who were once so exhilarated by the idea of living

the single life in Boston, backpacking through Europe, or starting their own businesses. Every passion became overshadowed
by the urgency to find a man. Many of my friends' mothers were
talking about wedding options, their fathers were giving the
stamps of approval on prospective husbands, and they all
seemed to know precisely which China pattern they could not
live without.

One of my closest friends, Carrie, who had wanted to be a
physician since the third grade, fell in love with a man who
balked at her interest in Women's Studies. Instead of registering
at medical school, she was registering at Bloomingdale's.

I saw nothing wrong with getting married someday, and I was
genuinely happy for my friends who were getting engaged. I just
couldn't understand what the rush was all about. Most of us
were only twenty-one! I also couldn't understand why I wasn't in
on the whole thing, why I lacked the desire to start my own
search for the perfect guy. Many of my friends thought I was in
denial and that I really wanted to get married, but was just trying
to be a "hard-core feminist." I started to wonder if they were
right. Maybe there was something wrong with me.

In February of my senior year, on a typically cold and drizzly
New England winter day, I received a call from my mother. My
grandma had died. This was the grandma who had always told
me to follow my dreams no matter how much other people
might discourage me. This was the woman who divorced her
husband in the 1930s and chose to pursue a life worthy of herself
and her daughter, despite the fact that in those days a divorced
mother might just as well resign herself to spinsterhood. This
was the woman who conquered the world in her own way, and
who always believed that I could conquer the world too if I
wanted. Now she was gone. Who else would believe me when I
said I didn't want to get married without thinking I was somehow defective as a young woman?

My father and I flew to Michigan for the funeral. We didn't

talk much on the plane, and my grief kept coming in waves the entire flight. I was exhausted from crying. In the car on our way to the church, I kept wishing I could talk to my grandma again. I had never felt so insecure about my feelings, and about my plans for the future. She would know exactly what to say. I started talking to her in my head, asking her what she would think if I chose not to get married. I hadn't realized that I was mumbling this conversation aloud until my father leaned over and said, "What did you say, Amy?"

I was startled. "Oh, nothing," I replied. What could my father have to say to me about marriage? He had walked happily down the aisle with my mother forty years ago, and had proudly accompanied three of my sisters at their weddings. No matter how hard I tried, I couldn't see myself as a bride, and I didn't want to imagine what a disappointment I would be if he didn't get the chance to give me away. When we arrived at the church, I didn't want to get out of the car and face the reality that my grandma was gone. I kept trying to talk to her, hoping that she would somehow answer me. In desperation, I suddenly turned to my father and asked, "Dad, would you be upset if I never got married?"

To my surprise, my dad laughed. He looked over at me, reached for my hand and said, "Of course I wouldn't be upset if you never got married. Marriage has been great for me, but that's because I married your mother. All I want is for you to live your life the way you want to live it, for you to be surrounded by people who love you always, and that you never stop gaining knowledge."

I could hardly speak. It was as if my grandma was there, nodding in agreement with my father, walking with us into the church. Those brief but reassuring words gave me the courage to stand at my grandma's funeral and tell everyone how much I loved her, and how much I looked forward to leading the life she always wanted me to lead—my own.

Four months after graduation and seven months after the funeral, I had my passport and work-abroad visa, and my bags were packed. As I boarded the plane for London, I looked back at my father, smiled, and waved goodbye. I never saw him so proud of me, and somehow I knew my grandmother was there too, applauding to the beat of my heart.

AMY JOHNSON

REGIE THE BEAR

I *was not looking forward to my first day in fifth grade* at St. Somebody's. I'd lost track of the names of elementary schools our many moves had occasioned. The pattern was consistent, though. My mom, my grandmother, and I would move to a new city, find an apartment, and enroll me in a new school—always a St. Somebody's. Gran would start a small business, it would fail, and we'd move on. I'd grown used to rarely being in a school long enough to buy a uniform.

So when students around me moaned when their names and mine were called to form a single line in front of Sister Regis, it didn't mean much to me. Sister Regis looked like an old salt. Her starched wimple seemed to have gathered all her excess flesh and distributed it in folds around her ruddy face. Thick yellow lenses magnified her pale eyes. In one hand she held a clicker, in the other the roster that sealed our doom.

It soon became apparent that Sister Regis had an extremely low tolerance for ten-year-olds. Her classroom rule was nothing short of tyrannical. She addressed us by our full Christian names. I became "Kathleen Mary," which she announced to the class would make a fine nun's name. She even renamed the two students in the class unfortunate enough to have names not listed in *Lives of the Saints*. Unknown to Sister Regis, we had changed her name, also. We called her Regie the Bear.

By October, two amazing things had occurred. The first was that I had a best friend. Mary Ann Caputo and I sat next to each other from the first day of school, and something clicked be-

tween us. She lived in the building next to ours, and we soon became inseparable. Gran called us the "double trouble twins."
And for the first time in my elementary school career I was popular. Sad to say, this popularity did not arise from my sterling aca-
demic performance, or my irresistible charm. It started with a
chant I had composed about Sister Regis:

*Regie the Bear, Regie the Bear, snappin' and a spittin' in her under-
wear.*

Laughing until we cried, classmates chanted it while playing
ball or jumping rope. We whispered it to one another while in
line or when sitting in the pews at first Friday Mass. Wherever
Sister Regis was not, my chant was sure to be heard.

While my popularity with the kids rose, my worth in Sister
Regis's eyes declined. I don't believe she ever heard the chant,
but she never missed my whispers to my classmates, my passed
notes, or my giggling during quiet times. I spent much of my
after-school time writing "God sees me" five hundred times,
punishment for one of my various classroom infractions.

Most of all, I believed Sister's animosity toward me revolved
around a more devastating character flaw. Whenever Sister asked
how many of the girls wanted to be nuns, I never raised my
hand.

"Well," she said one day, looking at me through a sea of flut-
tering hands, "and do you have something more profound in
mind than serving the Lord, Kathleen Mary?"

"No, Sister," I muttered. Then I looked at Mary Ann and
giggled.

"Perhaps you'll be a clown, Kathleen Mary," Sister growled.

From then on, I did my best to fulfill Sister Regis's prophecy.
For the first time ever, I liked school. I relished my classmates'
surrounding me as soon as I set foot on the school grounds in
the mornings. I always made sure I had a new joke or riddle to
share. Making people laugh became my priority. Best of all, my
friendship with Mary Ann grew like a precious flower.

Then, a week after New Year's Day, Gran announced after dinner one night that she had something to tell us. Mom, who suffered from a mental illness, wore a bland expression. My face crumpled. I'd heard it all before.

"I'm sorry, Kathy," Gran said, "someone bought the building where the business is. The new owner is doubling the rent. I just can't make it there."

Gran's latest business venture was a little café in the warehouse part of town. I knew it wasn't doing well, but I prayed each night that she could hold on a little longer, at least until I finished my magical fifth-grade year.

"I've talked to Uncle Joe in Gary," Gran continued. "He knows someone who's selling a diner, cheap. There's some apartments right nearby."

I knew better than to make a scene—we never did anything to upset Mom. I pushed away from the table, went to my room, and cried.

Even Sister Regis seemed aware of the change in my behavior throughout the following school week. I didn't tell a single joke. Not once did I join in on the Regie the Bear chant, and I couldn't bring myself to tell Mary Ann I was leaving.

"Are you mad at me?" she whispered that Friday after the dismissal bell.

I shook my head.

Mary Ann bounced up. "Don't tell me, then. See if I care."

If Sister Regis noticed I did not leave with the others, she didn't mention it. After she led out the silent line formed by my classmates, I put my head on my desk and sobbed—big wrenching sobs like I couldn't let out at home. I don't know how long it was before Sister returned and gathered me into the folds of her habit. She didn't say a word until the last of my shudders subsided. From somewhere in the depths of her robe, she pulled a handkerchief, handed it to me, and ordered me to blow.

Before I could think about it, I poured out the whole story to

Sister Regis, how badly I wanted to stay, how I finally had a friend, how I wondered if God even heard my prayers. All the while, Sister listened, nodded, patted my hand, wiped my eyes. When I finished, she gave me a brief hug.

"I'll pray for you, Kathleen Mary," she said. "And remember, your light will shine wherever you find yourself."

I couldn't get into my homework that night. What was the point? Even if I got an F, I'd be long gone before report cards came out. I'd just decided to call Mary Ann when someone knocked on our door. That's probably her, coming to apologize, I thought. I opened the door to Sister Regis.

"Good evening, Kathleen Mary," she said, swishing into the living room.

I couldn't stop staring. We'd never had a nun in our apartment before. Gran came in from the kitchen, wiping her hands on a towel. She'd met Sister Regis at a parent conference, but she looked as surprised as I was to find her in our living room.

"I hope I haven't come at a bad time," Sister Regis said to Gran. "I need to speak with you. Kathleen Mary, don't you have homework to do? This doesn't concern you."

Even through our thin apartment walls, I never heard one word Sister Regis said to Gran that night. But after she left, Gran came into my room and told me that she and Sister Regis felt it was very important for me to finish fifth grade in that school. In order to help that happen, Gran had accepted a job in the convent kitchen.

Things seemed different at school after that night. I still groaned along with the rest of the class when Sister clicked her clicker, stared us down, or assessed the standard five hundred "God sees me" penalty. But I didn't join in the chant anymore; eventually, it just faded away. Mary Ann and I remained friends.

Come June, Mom, Gran, and I moved to Gary, and I enrolled at another St. Somebody's. Mary Ann and I promised to write every day, but those letters faded out altogether by the time we'd moved from Gary, in the middle of sixth grade.

Two things sustained me during the ensuing years of change and turmoil—the remembrance of Sister Regis's hug, and her promise that my light could shine wherever I found myself. And so it has.

KATHLEEN M. MULDOON

In the stillness, there is dancing.
SUE DYER

OTHER DANCES

My brother asked me, when I was home from New York between dancing engagements two years ago, whether I ever secretly wished for an injury that would end my ballet career. He was in high school at the time, and a talented athlete in whom college scouts had showed much interest. I didn't know how to respond; I often wished that the pressure to land "the" job would subside, but never that my body would sustain an injury that would eliminate me in one blow from the long list of would-be principal ballerinas.

A week later, as I was running barefoot on the oceanfront, the rotator in my right hip tore. I was scheduled to depart for a winter-long tour of *The Nutcracker* and *Swan Lake* across Western Europe in two weeks. Eighteen years of hard work and waiting for the opportunity to perform *Swan Lake,* my favorite ballet, were suddenly over. And as my brother suspected, I was somewhat relieved.

For a long time, I'd felt at odds with the ballet world, but I was afraid to leave without ever having been the Swan Queen. Dance was not to blame for my frustrations; I'd been a willing student of it my whole life. What I really desired was a break with everything I'd known for the sake of a clean slate, but I didn't know how to go about it. Though I was afraid of what I might find, I decided to think of my injury as an opportunity to reinvent myself.

While in college, I'd cultivated other interests. I loved to learn languages, and to write fiction that evolved from years of compulsive letter writing. My brother used to watch me write letters to pen pals all over the world, one time saying, "I think you'd rather write than dance." He'd shake his head when I would jump up from the kitchen table late for rehearsal.

I thought of my brother's comment as I walked to and from the physical therapist's office for ultrasound treatments for the next month. I now had time to participate in the everyday events that my friends and family used to tell me about after I came home from the studio late at night. While recuperating, I found myself racing to the nearest library with drafts of handwritten stories on legal pads peeking out of my old dance bag. In time, the pain in my hip lessened, and I thought about going back to the studio as a teacher or choreographer.

Instead, I decided to choreograph and dance in a new way through my writing, new only because it took so long for me to realize that I'd been dancing on paper for as long as I had been dancing on stage.

Just as my brother was gearing up for the lacrosse season that would send him to a Division I school, I had opened the doors to my own enchanted kingdom, the one that lay hidden beneath my tiara for eighteen years, waiting to be discovered.

PAOLA JUVENAL

PROM DREAMS

The double doors leading to the delivery room swung open wide as my gurney was pushed through. All around me were huge bright lights and intimidating surgical instruments. *I shouldn't be here.* I kept thinking. *I'm only fifteen years old; I should be in school today. This can't be happening to me!* The pain was unbearable, but even more unbearable was the pain I caused my parents.

I was too ashamed to tell my mother I was pregnant, so she didn't find out until I was six months along. She hugged me and told me she loved me, but I knew I'd broken her heart and shattered her dreams of all she'd wished for me.

When I woke up in the hospital room after giving birth, Mom was next to my bed rocking my baby girl. I noticed the expression on my mother's face was one of mixed emotions. Her face told a story, one with a beginning and an end. It was a story that I understood later, after experiencing life.

As I lay in bed with my body and soul aching, the reality of the tremendous consequence, burden, and responsibility that was now mine was overwhelming. I closed my eyes to shut out the world around me. For a brief moment, I was riding horses with my sister on our five-acre ranch in Florida. I could hear our parents calling us in for supper. I pictured myself in gymnastics class, building a foundation for my dance career that included plans to own my own studio. A hungry baby's cry forced me back into the present. For now, the past was gone, along with my dreams.

The next several weeks were challenging, leaving me with a void in my life that I wanted to fill. When my daughter's father asked me to marry him, I was certain this was what I needed to complete me.

But my fairy-tale marriage was short-lived. While I was home day and night with my crying, colicky baby, I found out my husband was "dating" my best friend. My other friends were busy too, with dances and football games. My life had become dirty diapers, formula, and doctor visits. Although I dealt with what life had to offer me, I often caught myself daydreaming. I wondered what the inside of a high school campus looked like. I thought about the themes schools used to decorate for proms and imagined my date picking me up. I would never have a prom night like the other kids.

Just three months after I turned seventeen, my second baby—a boy—was born. Shortly thereafter, my ex–best friend gave birth to my husband's child.

I knew I couldn't support myself and my babies with only an eighth-grade education. My dad and stepmother, living in Florida, offered me a hand up—not a handout. For nearly a year, my son and daughter and I lived with them. I tended to the kids, kept house, and cooked dinner for my parents after their busy workday. My dad enrolled me in night school and watched the children for me while I earned my GED.

The State of Florida offered to put me in a special training program rather than on the welfare rolls. I chose nursing. Many days and nights it felt as though I wouldn't make it. If I studied hard enough, I could eventually memorize the technical terms, but the math had to be understood. Without four years of high school math as my foundation, I had to repeat several classes to keep up. My babies were sometimes sick, and my car often broke down on a lonely stretch of highway coming home from school at night. With my divorce pending, I was emotionally and physically exhausted.

Then, on a beautiful day in early June, my family and friends gathered at a little chapel in St. Augustine, Florida, to see me graduate from nursing school and receive my LPN license. As I walked down the aisle during the commencement ceremony, I noticed my loved ones had tears of pride, joy, and even some relief in their eyes. They knew how far I'd come from where I'd been.

My family continued to celebrate at Daytona Beach for a whole week, but I could only go for the weekend. Monday morning, I had to report for work at a nursing-care facility in my hometown.

Years later, as I sit having my morning coffee, I know I have come full circle with the choice I made and the consequence I paid. And time really *does* heal all wounds. Very soon now, I will be chaperoning my baby girl's high school dances and helping to decorate for her prom.

PAM THOMPSON

PAINTING TREES

*I*slunk out of the classroom with the rest of the students, as silent and horrified as if I'd just witnessed a gruesome car accident. Actually, what I'd been through felt far worse. It was a lethal calculus exam.

My friend Cindy sensed my dark mood.

"How did you do?" she asked hesitantly as we walked down the stairs out of the building.

"Terrible! Terrible! I have no idea what that test was even about! The questions came out of nowhere. I studied, but I might as well have been studying Latin."

Cindy offered sympathy, but I was too shocked and dejected to discuss it further. I had been getting fine grades in class, but I felt increasingly frustrated as I began to loathe the subject I had once loved. What was I doing as a math major anyway? The university had wanted me to pick a major, and I had—and math had seemed like a good idea at the time—but how was I truly supposed to know what I wanted to do already? I was still adjusting to college, far from ready to pick my life's career.

When Cindy and I emerged from the stifling structure that smelled like calculators and aging textbooks, the world opened up. The day was gorgeous, the kind of bright, colorful day that brings the university's public relations people out in droves to take as many promotional photos as possible before the real weather of Syracuse, New York, sets in.

As we walked across Syracuse University's quad, a flowery-scented breeze rustled the trees' green leaves. Students strolled to class, played Frisbee, and sat basking in the sunshine. Then I noticed a scattering of students with oversized white canvases, paintbrushes, and tubes of paint with names like alizarin crimson, cadmium yellow, and cobalt blue. They were "in class," capturing the beauty outside on canvas. My revelation smacked me like a belly flop into a swimming pool.

"I want to paint trees!" I suddenly screamed, startling Cindy.

"What?" She looked confused and somewhat frightened.

"I want to paint trees!" I repeated with gusto, my voice loud and rebellious. "Look at these students! I'm in there taking a hideous calculus exam and they're *painting trees!* Why can't I paint trees? I was not meant to be a math major. That's it. I've had it. I'm changing my major."

Soon after making my decision, I was sitting in the career services office staring at a computer that was supposed to tell me my destiny. You punch in your interests and abilities, and it spits out possible professions. Unfortunately, as far as tree painting goes, I'm not much of an artist. I knew I'd never make a living at it. But I had to change my direction, and fast!

After I was through being as picky as possible about what I would and would not do, the computer came up with a small, feeble list of possible careers for me. Only one sounded appealing: editor. Okay, I could see myself as an editor. I signed up to change majors and colleges and transfer into the communications school. My new major was "magazine journalism."

I pursued writing with much more enthusiasm than I'd ever had for calculus. I found a wonderful mentor, excelled in my classes, and eventually became a class marshal for the communications school. I would soon graduate with high honors in the company of dear friends. My choice had given me so much—but there was just one more thing I had to do before graduation.

The last semester of my senior year, I signed up for Painting and Drawing for Non-Art Majors. It was my chance to paint trees! As happily satisfied as I already was, taking this class gave me a burst of renewed excitement about life. Eagerly I wandered the aisles of the art-supply warehouse store, choosing paint tubes that oozed with brilliant color, soft sable brushes, and ivory drawing paper bursting with potential. I was ready to create a masterpiece. Well, at least I had the supplies for it.

Of course, masterpieces rarely develop for novices simply by their playing in pools of sticky color. In fact, I struggled with the class on many occasions. My drawings were never quite right, and an assignment on perspective led me to rework my project so many times that my eyes began to cross. Creating art is harder than it looks, I realized. I didn't think I was as talented as the rest of the class, yet somehow it didn't matter.

One afternoon as I traced lines of color down my canvas, the sunlight streamed through the giant panels of glass in our third-story rotunda room overlooking the campus. I watched the leaves on the trees flutter and studied the perfect blue sky. It was a day much like the one that had given me the spark to change my life's direction. I smiled at my good fortune: The weather was beautiful again, I was about to graduate, and I'd finally taken an art class.

Graduation came and went, and although I never became an artist, I know this for certain: The oak tree I painted in my final days at college was more than an amateur's simple vision of nature. It was my reminder that I could capture the life I wanted from the world outside and make it my own—as real as the brushstrokes on my page.

ALAINA SMITH

The secret to cheating death
is learning how to really live.
CECILIA MAIDA

IN SEARCH OF MERMAIDS

*O*n clear, crisp evenings when the stars appear so close you could reach up and touch them, I cannot help but think of Annabelle Wilson. Waiflike, almost ethereal, Annabelle seemed to float into our high school creative writing class in 1970. Swathed in voluminous dresses, her long hair pinned in a chignon, she seemed almost magical to us ninth-graders. We knew she was a graduate student, but she seemed younger than we were—too innocent, too wide-eyed, and too trusting.

"Write what you feel, write what's in your heart," she used to say to us. "Never be afraid to reach for the stars. Touch them for those who cannot."

Born in her mother's midlife, Annabelle was named for her two grandmothers—both had left this world long before her birth. Even her own father had died before she reached her second birthday. My mother used to say that change-of-life babies were extraordinary. As they had been with God for so long waiting to be born, they took a piece of heaven with them when they arrived here on earth. I had never paid much attention to my mother's tales, but with regard to Annabelle, I sensed she may have been on to something. In my mind's eye, I can still see Annabelle standing near an opened window, catching rays of sunlight. She looked almost translucent—somewhere between this world and the next.

Annabelle stayed with us throughout the year, painting pictures with her words. She had an uncanny way of unleashing the creative talents in the most unlikely candidates: Karl Jurgenson, who still works in the service station owned by his grandfather, writes poetry in his spare time. Lisa Anne Puleo, who married and produced five children within six years of our high school graduation, claims writing short stories has preserved her sanity, and Richard Bodekowski, who enlisted in the U.S. Marine Corps at eighteen, still keeps a daily journal, where he "writes what he feels and touches the stars every day." And each one of them credited their creativity to Annabelle's influence.

When Annabelle left us in June, there was no doubt in our minds that she would go on to write the proverbial great American novel, a five-act play worthy of a Tony, or a slim volume of exquisite poetry. At the very least, she would continue to inspire others by teaching creative writing—twirling about the room in delight as a student recited an opening paragraph.

But Annabelle would not write that book, pen that play, create that poetry, or even teach that writing class for a long time. That summer, her mother developed Alzheimer's disease and required constant care. Annabelle needed money quickly.

Putting her creative dreams on hold, she landed a job in a high-powered advertising firm. I could not imagine her within those corporate corridors housed in a downtown glass skyscraper. I could not visualize her developing slick brochures, editing corporate jargon, and promoting superficial merchandise. Every time I saw that office tower, I thought of it as a steel cage that imprisoned a beautiful wild bird.

Ironically, I landed a new job in that same building some ten years later. During my first week, I had wanted to visit Annabelle. I hadn't seen her since the ninth grade. But with all the confusion of starting a new job, I had postponed the visit. That weekend, while reading the morning newspaper, I noticed an obituary. Annabelle's mother had died. That Monday, I walked into Annabelle's office before my own. I needed to offer my condolences. I needed to see her.

When the elevator left me off on the sixteenth floor, I walked through the glass doors and located her cubicle. Several of her coworkers were milling about the area, shaking their heads. "We can't believe it. She just left. Why would she resign now? She knew she was going to be promoted this week."

As I looked at the pitiful gray cubicle that had housed Annabelle for the past decade, I cringed. A cold, drab prism, that had barely enough room for a metal desk and a straight-back chair. There were no windows, there was no sunlight, and these so-called coworkers who had spent ten years with Annabelle were genuinely confused. While they continued to ruminate about how could she have left, I kept asking how she ever stayed. Even more disturbing to me now was the question of what had happened to her during this ordeal. Had ten years in this quasi-prison broken her spirit? When I thought of her pirouetting in delight through our ninth-grade classroom, my eyes filled with tears.

While attempting to blink them away, I stared up at the ceiling. At first, it was difficult to discern, but they were there. Five tiny gold stars pasted on the ceiling above the cubicle. Seeing them, I smiled, and somehow knew at that very moment that Annabelle was okay.

"Where has Annabelle gone?" asked a voice I initially did not recognize as my own. "She's gone to search for mermaids, ride winged horses, and touch the stars." I am certain her former coworkers thought I was crazy, but I knew no one in that ninth-grade class back in 1970 would ever doubt me.

BARBARA DAVEY

BUTTERFLIES AND
ELEPHANTS

Seven hundred faces stared at me. *Some people* were tittering, others quietly attentive. Gowned in white dotted swiss and ruffles, I stood onstage. I was one of six girls in the senior class who had been voted "princess" to represent our high school in a huge, citywide festival. When I was selected, I knew that I'd eventually have to give a speech to the student body, so with a lot of trepidation, I decided to take on the challenge and conquer my fear of public speaking!

Little did the audience know that as I stood there looking "all together," my heart beat a staccato tattoo. Then I decided that must not be true at all—surely, they could hear the hammering of my heart. *Dear God, what am I doing?*

No butterflies remained in my stomach. No, now I had elephants! The thundering herd was threatening to trample me from the inside out. Nervousness filled my veins, making me light-headed.

Stepping to the microphone, aware of all the heads bobbing in the sea before me, I began. A few phrases tumbled out quickly, the tremor in my voice noticeable. Yet with the crowd quieted down, a growing sense of confidence began to build as each word left my mouth. My muscles relaxed. My breathing eased. Maybe the weeks of practicing before my bedroom mirror were paying off. *Maybe I can really do this,* I thought.

So much for my onstage vacation. Disaster struck as quickly as a rainstorm in the Bahamas! At first, all I knew was that the amplified sound of my voice had become distant. Like an echo you were supposed to hear but couldn't quite.

Just thirty seconds into my three-minute speech, and the microphone died. Glaring at the offending instrument of my potential downfall, I wondered if it was possible to strangle an inanimate object!

How could it do this to me?

Outwardly paralyzed with horror and humiliation, I frantically plotted the appropriate reaction. Should I run from the stage in despair, or wait for power to return to the microphone? Time seemed to stand still, crystallizing a moment of opportunity—when intent suddenly meant everything.

So I chose neither of my first all-too-quick solutions. After all, how could I be the victor if I didn't face this unexpected obstacle head-on?

Making the next moment my own, I closed my eyes, to still my quaking limbs, being thankful for a long dress. I next forced out the hot anxiety in my lungs, to make room for what I intended to do.

One deep inhale, one moment . . . and then I continued. Before me, the hushed audience focused on each new word, as if I was a bird, singing out for the very first time. Knowing I had made the right decision, I felt the blood return to my drained face, along with a calm, sure feeling. And from somewhere beside myself, I heard my voice boom, this time without electronic help. It reached far into the recesses of the upper balcony, where I could see people no longer bobbing their heads, but sitting rapt, maybe astounded at my tenacity.

My soliloquy ended. It was a moment in time I could always call my own, no matter how they responded. Then the cheering began, surging into a thunderous response. I watched, still surprised, as students rose to their feet, the large room actually vibrating with applause.

Humble on the outside, my heart nearly burst with pride on

the inside. I had mastered my greatest fear, along with a big extra dose of unforeseen adversity. I'd faced my butterflies and even elephants of anxiety. Now, as I looked out on the audience, I thought, this loud cheering is a *new* kind of elephant thundering in my ear!

Then a realization swept over me like a gift. In an instant, I knew—*I could do anything!* Taking a bow in my white dotted swiss, I felt a glow that I'll never forget, knowing that within me existed a young woman once tested. A young woman bolder than her fear.

LISA ROBERTSON

VI
KEEPING THE HIGH WATCH

Help me stay in touch with my soul no matter what.

Susie Troccolo

GETTING BACK ON

*E*arly in the spring I turned nine, I graduated from riding my pony to my first horse. I'd prayed for months for this miracle and slept with the smell of saddle soap, leather oil, and pony sweat on my palms. When I heard the rattle of the trailer coming down our long drive, I could hardly stand still as the seller unloaded my new companion.

From the beginning, Babe surprised me. Instead of the wispy, flowing mane and tail I expected, her mane was cropped short. A horsy mohawk ran from her ears to her withers, and her tail hair was chopped just below the bone. Her coat was a dull white and her neck and girth thick. Sturdy, you might say. My dream horse wasn't sturdy, but fine-boned, with magical strides so fluid under me that a trot or a canter would feel equally comfortable. Babe wasn't my dream horse at all.

Once the seller left, I took Babe for our first ride. My pony saddle didn't fit, so I went bareback. Although Babe's strides were a little jerky, her back sat soft and comfortable. Halfway up the long gravel road, leading from our house at the bottom of the hill, we paused. I had planned to turn around at the spot where the blackberries thickened, but Babe was doing so well, I decided to ride to the top of the rise. As I turned her at the peak, she suddenly took off at a full gallop down the hill!

I am going to die. This horse is crazy!

I grabbed for mane to hang on to and found nothing but prickly mohawk, then I put my arms around her thick neck and hung on, watching the gravel whip by beneath me. We made it to the bottom of the hill, and just when I thought I was safe, I slid off right under her. A thousand pounds of horse stomped on my left hand. I curled into a ball and sobbed.

About half an hour later, after lots of ice and tears, when the pain eased and Mom and Dad knew my hand wasn't broken, Mom said, "Now you have to go get back on her." Plain and simple she said it, as if she was telling me to wash up for supper or clean my room.

Now Mom's crazy, I thought. *How can she make me get back on?* Well, she did. "That's how you conquer your fears and get over your falls," she said. After a time, I got back on because there was no other way. I prayed to God to keep me safe as I climbed, shaky, back on.

That first summer, as Babe's mane and tail grew out, we galloped through the neighborhood, a bandanna tied over my face and a cowboy hat on my head, as I pretended to chase Indians.

One fall, when the days were beginning their rush toward darkness, we wound through a forest dappled with the reds and golds of maple and oak. The gentle whir of the river we paralleled put us both in a peaceful daze. Near dusk, we came to a fork in the trail. I realized we were lost. I wrapped my arms around Babe's neck and whispered, "You pick," then nudged her forward with my heels. Sure enough, her instincts brought us home.

Babe's ears were always alert and perky. She loved to explore and insisted on being in front when other horses and riders joined us. The two of us constantly searched for long, soft straightaways to gallop full-tilt. The stretch of her neck and the speed as the sky, clouds, ground, and trees blurred by left me exhilarated and grateful to Babe for giving me her all. At those times, nothing else existed but me and my horse, racing gracefully as fast as we could.

During the winters, I kept Babe draped in her blanket to ward off the frost and to keep her white coat clean. For Christmas dinners, I brought her apple, carrot, and sugar salad.

Summer brought hours of practice for horse shows and fairs, but Babe didn't care, she was invariably ready for that next go-round, and the endless grooming of her now flowing mane and tail.

At the county fair during our last year together before Babe died, she held her head high, mane and tail streaming, knowing she was a champion, and we won Grand Champion in Stockseat Equitation. We hadn't always been champions; it took time for us to grow together, learn each other's rhythms, and meld them into one fluid whole. As we took our victory lap around the ring, it suddenly hit me. Babe and I had spent six years growing up together. And if I hadn't gotten back on her all those years before, I would have missed all the fun and all the glory—and the knowing that she was my dream horse after all.

KRISSA ENGLEBRIGHT

As soon as I opened to God, things just fell into place.
CHRISTINA APPLEGATE

ASK AND YOU SHALL RECEIVE

A rash of brutal rapes took place on the university campus I attended in the late 1980s. And while the suspect had been identified, he eluded capture. Posters with his picture hung in every building, and the administration enacted a strict curfew in an effort to prevent further attacks. In fact, as one young woman, an acquaintance of mine, left the library alone that night, she walked right past his face on the wall with the warning written above it: "Contact campus police immediately if you spot this man."

Completely alone, she stepped into the crisp night air. The park and the pathways were deserted as students took shelter in their dorms from the prevailing sense of dread. Not wanting to be a sissy, she hurried down the library's stone stairs. She could cut through the park and be home in under five minutes. What could happen in under five minutes, she reasoned?

She sensed him before she actually saw him, lurking behind the big oak tree behind her halfway down the path. Swiftly he stepped onto the pavement and closed the distance between them. Unarmed, unprepared, and utterly alone, she did the only thing she'd ever known to do when gripped by fear.

"Dear God," she prayed quietly as she quickened her pace, "keep me safe. Please God, help me."

She walked and prayed, walked and prayed, the whole time aware of his presence not fifteen feet behind her. Finally at home, she climbed the stairs to her dormitory and found safety inside.

Based on her tip, the police quickly located the suspect and escorted her that very night to identify him at the police station. As she left to return home, she saw him sitting, handcuffed at a desk while he was being questioned. Knowing better, yet overcome with curiosity, she approached the man.

"You didn't hurt me," she said. "Why didn't you hurt me?"

"How could I?" the man answered sarcastically. "I'd have been crazy to try anything with you after that big man crossed over the road and walked with you all the way home."

ELLEN URBANI HILTEBRAND

MY MOTHER AFTER ALL

I can see it in the attic photos, page by page,
all our mother-daughter memories,
all the years and all the growing that was ours.
I can feel it in the denim dress
you made for me at five.
It matched yours beautifully,
So I wore it with a daughter's pride.

I can taste it still, the love you put,
in all the casseroles and cakes,
teaching me that I could cook—
using one part joy and one part patience—
when I was only seven
but thought I must be eight.

I can feel it, from the inside,
as you drove me to softball games—or was it to ballet?
No matter my performance,
you always found a way to make me feel
that I was more than fine, that I was simply great.

I can hear it, all too quickly, by thirteen,
the sound of all of me—
too cool to love you, too hip to be you,
too busy for your endless chores and lists.

I became so involved with making me,
I was sure you didn't quite exist.

I can recall it, like yesterday,
grounded from my freedom all too often at sixteen,
I fought your structure and your limits
with the energy of the rebel that I'd found.
"I never want to be like you,"
I spoke boldly so you'd know,
but you spoke back softly, with a smile of wiser years,
"It's unavoidable, my daughter"—
but I pretended not to hear.

I can remember it all too well,
at seventeen you held my hand
as heartbreak held me all too fast.
You said, "Remember all the good times,
then let go. Love is worth it
and I know, someday it will come back."

I can feel the car wheels as they rolled
all so quickly away from home,
But as surely as the college miles were far
the closer to you did I grow—
at first creating lists, then acting with a new enthusiasm
instead of giving up or giving in.

Now, as I look around my house
I chuckle instead of yell.
From the closet, down to every hook
and shoe pile, to every tidy file—
this house is mine,
but Mom, it really looks like yours!

I can see it all so clearly,
in the mirror, even our hair now looks the same.
But even more than all of that,
it's who I have become today.
I can see how deep within myself
there is a loving sigh
as I mimic your compassion
and it gives me quiet pride.

And I feel your dedication, Mom,
to stick things through until the end.
After all these years, you're more than a role model,
you're an inspiration . . . and a friend.

So when I find myself doing something like you now,
I hold my head quite tall.
With a peaceful smile, I realize
I've become my mother after all.

MARGUERITE MURER

A PRAIRIE TALE

*B*eing *the only child of a poor dry land farmer in* South Dakota provided few cultural opportunities or luxuries but a host of opportunities for the imagination. At an early age, my father helped me distinguish between schooling and learning. He'd readily point out that "a fool can have a degree but no common sense."

My father was a shy man, an intellectually curious man, and a man of principle. He explained poetry, geometric abstractions, and philosophy to me. He taught by example and through experience.

Each morning, beginning in first grade, he would call up to my room, "Nancer, are you going to school this morning?" Each day I was given the choice of learning at school or learning at home. The learning part was not an option! (Years later, I found out that Dad had talked with each teacher each year and drawn a bargain that as long as my grades were high, they promised to never ask why I hadn't been in school.)

If it was Monday, I almost always said, "Yes, I'll be right down." For that was the day we got the week's assignments mandated by the county curriculum. On Tuesday, I would go to school if my assignments weren't done. But usually on Wednesday and Thursday, if I attended school, I'd end up sitting in an uncomfortable desk reading Nancy Drew books all day waiting for Friday, when we had art.

Needless to say, I don't remember attending a full week of elementary school. Instead, I did field trips with my father (his version of home schooling). We would wander the creeks identifying leaves, trees, and animal tracks. He pointed out signs of the migration of animals and the distinguishing characteristics of poisonous plants.

After eight years in a one-room country school with five other classmates, no running water, and sawdust on the floor, I moved on to high school several miles away. I still got the same question each morning. "Nancer, do you want to go to school?" I found high school a lot more fun and socially more rewarding. As any teenager would, I wanted to be with my friends. So I often opted for a day at school instead of the creek.

After the first semester, Miss Dykstra, my principal, called me to her office. I felt very special because I admired her so. Each morning, she would bring the entire assembly to absolute silence with a principal-like look. Then she'd take attendance of the 104 students enrolled and proceed to announce the day's special events. I wanted to be just like her someday: confident, in charge, and respected by all.

I walked down the hall and up the five steps to Miss Dykstra's office. I was excited to have a private meeting with her. I tried to anticipate what she might say: "Your achievements in class are great," or maybe, "Your performance in the school play was outstanding." Maybe I'd won something.

The door was open to the principal's office. I stood at the entry until she noticed me and invited me in to sit down. Miss Dykstra was tall and thin. She wore serious suits and sensible shoes. Her features were fine, and she had a natural delicate country beauty, with short-cropped hair.

As I sat in the chair in front of her desk, she leaned forward and said, "Nancy, I've called you here to discuss your attendance." *Oh, so that's what this is about,* I thought. I was beaming with pride. She'd noticed! Then she continued. "You've missed twenty-two days so far this year."

I figured that was only about one day a week and I replied,

"Yes, Miss Dykstra, I really *like* high school! That's why I'm here so often!" A grin crossed her face; she'd gone to school with my father. She knew his philosophy: protect and nurture the love of learning. Yet she was duty-bound to discuss my attendance with me.

Barely able to keep from laughing, she sent me out of her office, down the steps, and back to study hall with, "I'm glad you enjoy high school and hope you remember learning never ends."

After high school graduation, the possibility of college was beyond my dreams and definitely beyond the household budget. The money I'd saved from waitressing in high school, however, could get me through a year of beauty school. After a month of cutting and curling hair, I was bored and desperate for more stimulation. I was a hundred miles from home and my parents did not have a phone. So I called Miss Dykstra. She was thrilled to hear from me and told me she'd pick me up in two hours. What I had not anticipated was that Miss Dykstra didn't drive me home, she drove me to the nearest college and enrolled me.

Along the way, I protested, "Who's going to pay for this?" She declared, "You are. Get another part-time job and check into student loans." So I did.

Today I'm a "beauty school dropout" with a BS, an MA, a Ph.D., and a habit of lifelong learning. Thanks to my father, who inspired my love of learning, and Miss Dykstra, who taught me the value of school attendance.

NANCY KIERNAN

There is no wisdom equal to that which comes after the event.
GERALDINE JEWSBURY

A LITTLE SISTER'S PRAYER

*M*y knees shook, and I was grateful that the podium hid them. Looking around at all those familiar faces, I tried to relax. I was among friends. I felt inspired to speak, but I didn't know if I'd find the right words to convey the experience I wanted to share.

It had been a simple enough assignment. My ninth-grade English teacher, Sister Mary Margaret, wanted each of us to give a speech on something interesting. We had a choice of reading a fully written speech or giving a talk based on an informal outline. It had been obvious from the whispers and giggles among the girls that our speeches would cover a variety of topics. Since talking was one of my favorite pastimes, I knew I would find something easy to discuss. As the three o'clock bell rang, I pushed thoughts of Sister Mary Margaret's assignment to the back of my mind. I didn't plan to think about it again until Sunday night.

I spent Saturday morning working as a cashier at my father's car wash. The time passed quickly, and before I knew it, Dad was suggesting hamburgers for lunch. We called ahead to order twelve hamburgers, four large orders of french fries, and enough drinks to satisfy the six hungry Gonzaleses waiting at home.

Everything smelled so delicious as Dad and I set the bags of food on the kitchen table. I quickly ran upstairs to my room to change my clothes and call my big sister, Chris, to lunch.

As I reached the top of the stairs, I heard a strange whimpering. I went into my bedroom, and realized the sound was coming from the bathroom that connected my bedroom to my sister's.

I called out, "Chris?"

I went into my room and knocked on the bathroom door, hoping one of her dogs was trapped in the bathroom, making that awful sound—that it wasn't . . .

Suddenly Mother yelled out my name. As I turned to leave my bedroom, I saw her run to the top of the stairs and call loudly, "Gilbert! Gilbert! Come up here! Hurry!"

As Daddy raced up the steps, I heard her yelling something about suffocation, the heater, and my sister. I was frozen to the spot where I stood.

I saw them running into my sister's bedroom. Even though I was frightened, I decided I had to see if I could help.

When I stepped into Chris's room, I saw that my parents had dragged my sister's body from the bathroom. She was covered in towels as they laid her near an open window. Her moaning and whimpering continued as my parents called her name and gently slapped her cheeks as they tried to bring her back to consciousness.

When my dad left Chris's side to telephone for an ambulance, I took his place and began to call her name as he had done. My mother asked me to help dress my sister in a robe. As we struggled with her lifeless body, I started to notice an unusual odor in the room and looked toward the bathroom

The door was in complete shambles. I looked into my mother's worried face and realized that she had broken the door down, reducing the wood to splinters and jagged pieces. Even though I don't remember her exact words, Mom told me about

the faulty heater and that my sister had fallen asleep in the bath-
tub. My mother had come to call her, when she had heard my
sister's moaning. She had no choice but to break down the door.

My father came back, and I decided to wait downstairs for the
ambulance. I was so scared to see my sister as she was. I felt so
powerless to help her.

My prayers that afternoon, as I sat waiting for the ambulance,
were the most dramatic of my young life. I prayed to God to
help my sister, not to let her die. Chris was my only sister, and
though I loved my five brothers, they could never replace all the
laughter, intelligence, and creativity that made Chris so special.

It seems as though I sat there on the front porch and prayed
for hours, even after the ambulance came and took Chris to the
hospital.

As long as I live, I will never forget the thick cloud of fear that
hung over the Gonzales home that day. My three younger brothers watched television quietly, with none of the usual fighting
over TV channels, or who should sit in Daddy's big chair. I saw
my older brother, Mike, stay home and watch over the rest of us,
something I hadn't seen since he'd bought his race car. Mike answered the phone and talked quietly to us. That afternoon, I believe we all became aware of how much we loved one another.

Chris came back home that night. My parents had saved her
from the gas in time to stop any carbon-monoxide poisoning,
and the doctors said that after a few days of rest, Chris would be
fine. I took my turn visiting Chris upstairs, and as I remember, it
was the first time I ever told her, "I'm so glad you're alive. I never
want anything bad to happen to you."

I recall that I went back to the kitchen later, where the bags of
cold hamburgers still remained on the table.

The following Monday, I gave my speech on the topic of "Sisters." Without any notes, I gave a speech from my heart.

On trembling legs, I admitted to my friends that I had taken
my sister for granted, and in one scary afternoon I had learned

how much she meant to me. I told them that on Saturday my sister had almost died and what I had realized from the experience. I spoke about the unique person who was my sister. And I finished by discussing the value of having a big sister.

When I finished talking, there was complete silence in the room. Had I touched a few guilty sisters out there? To this day, I don't know if I gave that speech for all those little sisters in the classroom, or if I was only talking for myself. All I know is that everything in the Gonzales home, and in the relationship between my sister and me would never be the same again.

Today I feel lucky that my big sister is also one of my best friends. And I'm thankful that on one very scary Saturday, God listened to a little sister's prayers.

DIANE GONZALES BERTRAND

Life is our schoolroom, . . . and love is always
the best teacher.
JOAN WALSH ANGLUND

IF I'D KNOWN THEN WHAT
I KNOW NOW

Recently when no one else was home, I sat down in my favorite cushy chair, closed my eyes, and got real quiet. The assignment I'd given myself was to let memories float into my mind of situations I'd change from my growing-up years if I'd known then what I know now. For each memory that surfaced, I hoped to get some learning. Some of the memories that surfaced didn't surprise me, but others did— events I hadn't thought of in a long time.

When my second-grade teacher announced a sign-up for an all-school talent contest, I half-danced, half-ran home to tell Mom. I remember her reaction confused me. "What will you do?" she asked. I didn't know yet, but somehow I sensed she was worried. That's when I began doubting myself for the first time. By the time I decided to tap dance to the same music we used in dance class, my unbridled enthusiasm had long since disappeared! I performed my routine on stage in fear. After that I never raised my hand in class, I never signed up for a speech class in junior high, high school, or college, and I would get embarrassed easily if a teacher called on me suddenly, catching me off guard. *If I'd known then what I know now, I'd let others keep their doubts, and I'd trust that I can do well with whatever I set my mind to.*

One day in junior high, nurses came to school to check everyone's scalps for lice. One popular girl in our class had them, and many of us ignored her from that day on. Just like that, she was no longer a part of our inner circle of friends. We didn't invite her to go places with us, share lockers, or call her at home. *If I'd known then what I know now, I'd know that the true test of friendship is not during the easy times but during the tough times.*

When I was a sophomore in high school, a new guy in school asked me to dance after a Friday night football game. He was a very cool dancer, and we mirrored each other's steps perfectly. The next night he called, and I made up a story that I was dating someone else. My heart wanted to say yes, but I found my voice saying no. I didn't have a clue what to do with my feelings for him. We never talked again. *If I'd known then what I know now, I'd have the courage to be honest with how I feel—it's much less complicated!*

In my senior year, I was wild about a boy named Bob. We went together all year but drifted apart after graduation. During college, a mutual friend called to say Bob was dying of leukemia in the hospital. I never went to see him. I couldn't think of what to say. *If I'd known then what I know now, I'd go sit on the edge of his bed, lean down, and whisper in his ear lyrics from our song, "I Wanna Be Bobbie's Girl," and thank him for being in my life.*

I can now see that in each of these experiences, I was holding back love, either for myself or for someone else. But it's not about the "mistakes" I made, it's about learning from them that counts.

With my heightened awareness, I closed my eyes again, went

back to each scene, and changed the endings, using what I know now. I opened my eyes and felt grateful for the learning. I now know that with each new situation I encounter, the most useful ingredient I can add to the mix is love.

KAY ALLENBAUGH

LITTLE GIRL, BIG GIRL

*I*help out with an elementary preschool program as part of my high school early-childhood-education class. Part of my job is sitting on the floor and reading with the kids.

One morning during a quiet time between teacher talk and the next story, Katrina discovered me alone on the floor and plopped down into my lap. When Katrina saw one of her friends close by, she said, "Chloe, come sit with us," and moved over to make space. Chloe got all comfy in my lap and popped her thumb in her mouth. Katrina glanced up at me, sat real tall, and said, "Sucking your thumb's such a baby thing."

Chloe's forehead wrinkled into a frown and her wet thumb slipped down into her lap where she held it with her other hand. I put my arm around Chloe, gave her a big squeeze, and said, "I still suck my thumb." Katrina checked to see if I was serious, then peeked at Chloe, once again sucking her thumb, all cozy and relaxed against my chest.

I whispered in Katrina's ear, "Go pick out a story." Katrina ran to the bookshelves, retrieved *Harold and the Purple Crayon,* then scooched back into my lap with Chloe. As Katrina settled in and the story began, her hand crept up near her face, and by the middle of Harold's adventures, her thumb found its way into her mouth.

RUTH ACHILLES

MORE THAN A TEST

I *can remember the day as if it were yesterday. I* was sitting in my apartment with my fiancé, Keith, cozied up to a warm fire. We were discussing our upcoming wedding plans, what kind of home we would like to live in, how many pets we would have, and of course the perfect job. The kind of job you'd enjoy going to every day.

Keith worked for the sheriff's department, and he seemed to think I would make a fantastic police dispatcher. I sat there for a minute wondering if I would be able to handle such a stressful job. As I listened to him speak of our future together, my becoming a police dispatcher suddenly started to sound good. And why not? I'd have great benefits, health coverage, and paid holidays. What more could I ask for?

While daydreaming about the possibility of us working for the same employer, I suddenly remembered something I was very ashamed of—I never graduated from high school, and I never received a high school diploma. I thought, *What will Keith think of me?* I knew we were always honest with each other, and I felt uncomfortable that I hadn't told him this before. My heart was beating fast, and I knew I had no other choice but to be honest.

"I need to tell you something about me—something that I've never told you. If I applied to get a job as a police dispatcher, they wouldn't hire me because I never graduated from high school. I fell in love and was so infatuated with the guy that school didn't matter to me. I didn't realize how important it was to get an education, and I dropped out my senior year." Tears ran down my face as I told him.

"Is there anything else I don't know about you?" Keith asked with a half smile.

"No, that's it," I answered between ragged breaths.

He took me in his arms and told me not to worry. Keith didn't judge me. He just loved me for who I was, and nothing else seemed to matter.

The next day, we drove to my favorite bookstore in the mall to look for a book that would prepare me for taking the General Educational Development tests so that I could receive my high school diploma. Keith bought me the book, saying, "I want to give you the gift of education."

My next step was to sign up at my local high school for an evening GED class. I was scared and didn't know what to expect. I was worried that I'd be the oldest one in class, or that I'd forgotten what I'd already learned in school. I was so anxious before the first class that out of desperation I asked myself, *What do you have to lose?* From then on, I was able to concentrate. I studied every night, hour after hour, day after day, and no one knew except Keith.

On test day, the questions were broken out into five parts: Writing Skills, Social Studies, Science, Interpreting Literature and the Arts, and Mathematics. I worked methodically through each section until I got to the math part of the test. I thought, *Oh my God, this has always been my toughest subject.* I knew I had to pray harder than I ever had before. I prayed continuously through all sixty questions. I stared at every question, hoping God would give me the answers! When my time was up, I put my pencil down, took a deep breath, and gathered up my things. I handed my exam to a friendly woman at the front desk and asked her to say a prayer for me too.

The drive home seemed to take forever. As I ran up the steps to my apartment, I heard the telephone ringing. Quickly unlocking the door, I raced to answer the phone. It was the woman from the front desk calling. She was so excited for me that when I left, she immediately put my exam into the computer to get my score. I closed my eyes and heard her say, "You did it! You got your GED!" I burst into tears, feeling really proud of myself. I shouted to Keith, "Honey, I did it!"

One look in his eyes, and I realized that Keith had given me more than the gift of an education—he had helped me to become more than I ever thought I could be.

VALENTINA A. BLOOMFIELD

THE WEDDING

Several months ago, my daughter Camille told me she was getting married. I was happy for her and her young man. He is a very nice guy with a promising future.

Last weekend, we went to try on wedding dresses. As I looked at Camille standing there, gazing at her reflection in the mirror, my mind wandered back to another time and place.

"Her eyes are beautiful," I remember my husband saying as the doctor laid her tiny body in my arms. I looked down at this precious miracle and smiled. Her eyes were black, like a starless night, and she had hair to match.

In the days that followed, I began to map out her life for her in my mind. She would turn many a young man's head with those dark features, but I would have to teach her that looks aren't everything. I would have to teach her that to succeed in life, she would have to work hard and be strong.

As she grew, I saw her personality take shape. She had an infectious grin bordering on mischievous. She was always running to keep up with her two brothers and sister. She was a determined little girl. I remember one day she was trying to stack some blocks. They kept falling. She was not discouraged, though, and kept trying again and again to stack them up. Finally, when the blocks were in a neat little pile, she turned to me with a triumphant smile. I knew then that she would not be a quitter.

"Mom, how does it look?" she asked me now, bringing me out of my reverie.

"It looks beautiful," I replied, smiling.

Looking at my woman-child in this gown of white satin and lace, I see a part of myself. I remember my own wedding day and how happy I was. I was still very young, but I knew it was right. I was in love. Now, some twenty years and five children later, my life has come full circle.

When I witness the marriage of my child, it will be with the hope that it is lasting. I have to believe that it will last forever. It will be a hectic few months, but I am ready for the challenge. I'm sure my daughter will have me running in circles, but I will try to stay calm. One of us has to.

I look forward to that last day of July when my daughter is standing at the altar with her intended. I will remember again that little girl trying to stack blocks on our living room floor, and her triumphant smile when she finally succeeded. I might even cry, but they will be tears of joy.

SHARON SCHAFER

VII
MAKING MEMORIES

No matter how long I live, there will never be a dull moment.

HARRIET DOERR

A day so soft you could wrap a baby in it.
MARCELENE COX

COMFORT IN THE WILD

T hey say elephants have great memories. I hope so. I hope he remembers.

I came across a baby elephant—not yet a week old—while on a game reserve in Zimbabwe. He had fallen into a water pump hole and couldn't get out. The herd had apparently stuck around for a couple of days trying to dig him out, but they weren't successful. They finally abandoned him.

A day or two later, when one of the park rangers went to check the pump, he found the despondent elephant staring up at him. He shoveled dirt for hours and, with a bit of water, coaxed the infant out.

That's when I met him. I had been on safari that day, and we decided to stop and eat under a thatched gazebo in the middle of the savanna. We had just unloaded the truck when the ranger walked up to us, baby elephant tagging along behind.

At first, I didn't know what to think. I'd never been so close to an elephant. I didn't know whether to be scared or curious, but his big glossy black eyes radiated warmth. He was scared and confused, lost among strangers, but he was a brave little guy. I suddenly felt a kinship to this youngster. I too felt scared and confused, lost among strangers. I'd been living halfway around the world for several months, and the novelty was starting to wear off. The adventure and the excitement had died down considerably, and I was beginning to long for a familiar face. But it wasn't time to go home, not just yet. My research project would keep me there the entire year, and I had a long haul ahead of me.

That afternoon, though, I made a friend. He stood only three feet tall, and I'd guess he weighed about 300 pounds. He moved with the clumsiness and curiosity of a toddler, stumbling over his large padded feet and flapping his oversized ears as if he thought he could fly.

I was elected caretaker for a few hours as the ranger and most of our group headed back to the base to find a veterinarian. While they were gone, the baby elephant followed me around in circles, nuzzling the back of my thigh with his trunk and slamming into me when I stopped. Every once in a while, he'd lift his trunk up and try to roar, but all that came out was a muffled honk. I knew how he felt, and it made me laugh.

By the time the guide returned with the vet and a special truck equipped with a cage, that little elephant and I had warmed up to each other, and I began to worry about what lay ahead for him.

I didn't have to wonder long. As the vet checked him over, he told me about plans to take him to an animal orphanage in Bulawayo, about 200 miles away. I'd been there, and it put my mind at ease to know that he'd be taken care of.

Still, I felt a lump forming in my throat as the vet loaded him into the cage, and the little guy reached out with his trunk as if to say goodbye. Short though our friendship was, I like to think it was genuine. For a few hours, we shared our lives, our loneliness, and our uncertainties, but for a few hours, we also found peace and comfort in each other's presence. As the truck's engine fired up, I gave my friend one last pat on the head, scratched him under his chin, and whispered, "Good luck, buddy. *Endo zvakanaka.* You stay strong, and so will I."

I wonder if he remembers.

DELIN CORMENY

THE BASKET LADY

Magical *things happen when we least expect* them. Sometimes they sit in our minds and twinkle for several years before we recognize them as magic at all. That's what the Basket Lady did for me.

The Basket Lady came not so gently one day into our home in 1956. Winters in Iowa are cold, snowy, and slippery. As my father held the back door open, a slight, gray-haired lady entered our home. She slid across the tiled entrance with an unusual flair and landed by the edge of the soft green carpet. Trying not to laugh, I ducked sway from a strange, brown basket that came spiraling through the air. It landed on its side, as did the lady. My father helped her up and made sure everything was in its right place. Her hat was tipped slightly, but her arms, legs, and other necessities appeared to be intact.

"Help with the basket, will you please, Kathie," my father said.

"Sure, Daddy," I responded, "but what is all of this?"

"Kathie, just put it back in the basket. I'm sure that Mrs. Armontrout will show you later."

"Do you promise?" I asked as I looked up at the quaint little lady with the strange name.

"Yes, I do," she said as she placed her feathered hat on the table and adjusted her glasses that had been tilted from the fall. "I have lots of favorite things in there. We'll take a look after your parents have left."

At five years old, I didn't like my parents to leave for the evening. I was usually bored whenever a babysitter stayed with me. Tonight felt different. I couldn't wait.

"Goodbye," Mother said as she gently kissed my sister Julie and me on the cheeks. "Now the two of you be good and go right to bed when Mrs. Armontrout tells you to."

Armontrout, I thought, as I heard the door close behind my parents. I think that we ate something like that the other night, but I couldn't be sure. It was a funny name, but somehow it fit. She had wispy gray hair that didn't seem to have any real pattern to it. I loved to comb other people's hair. *Maybe she'll let me do that late,* I thought, as I studied her upswept locks.

"Come on over and sit here beside me," the little lady said as she patted either side of herself on the couch. "I've got some special things to share with the two of you."

My older, more cautious sister was not in any hurry. She lingered across the room and finally sat on the corner of the floral couch in an unapproachable manner.

"Like me, Julie. Sit closer."

Julie inched her way over on the couch. It wasn't easy for her. As the evening progressed, Mrs. Armontrout became the frosting in our sandwich cookie—two girls with a sweet surprise in the center.

"It's very full," I observed, as I helped Mrs. Armontrout lift the basket to her lap.

"Full of my favorites."

"Your favorites. What are your favorites?" The pitch of my voice rose as the question flew from my mouth.

"Favorites are things that are special to you. They put smiles in your heart, dreams in your mind, and laughter on your lips. Favorites open doors and carry you to far away fantasies."

I did a double take of Mrs. Armontrout, as Julie's eyes shifted quickly from side to side. Was this lady for real, and if so, what was she talking about?

I was a little confused about what Mrs. Armontrout had told

us, but I found myself lingering on her every word. There were sparkles that seemed to radiate from her eyes and dance around my head with the gracefulness of a butterfly after a fresh spring rain.

All that evening and many more that were to follow, my sister and I would sit like bookends, on each side of Mrs. Armontrout. We delighted in stories of her favorite thimble, pencil, map, and key. We were enthralled by her sewing cards and puzzles, and her favorite books were soon to become my favorites too. We heard stories of Mrs. Armontrout's favorite foods and her favorite places to eat them. She even had a favorite dish for her rhubarb and one for her cornmeal mush.

Soon I didn't notice Mrs. Armontrout's frizzled hair, nor did her name sound so peculiar to me anymore. My imagination had been set free, and it filled my senses with purpose. The Basket Lady had given me something in later years I realized I could never buy. She had instilled in both my sister and me a wealth of imagination, beliefs, and values.

I don't know whatever happened to the Basket Lady. She stopped coming to babysit as my interests grew along with my adolescence. But I believe with all my heart that Mrs. Armontrout is in a special place, and that she watches me with my children and the students I teach, as I share favorites of my own.

KATHIE HARRINGTON

I suppose you can't have everything,
though my instinctive response to this sentiment is always,
Why not?
MARGARET HALSEY

MY CHRISTMAS WISH

orest-green and serene, our noble fir Christmas
tree stood in the corner of the living room, glittering
with ornaments. Lights, like tiny fireflies, cast colored
hues on bright shreds of wrapping paper scattered across the carpet and tumbling out of a large plastic bag. Only an hour before,
the barren space beneath the tree had been filled with presents.
Now all the presents had been opened.

My five-year-old eyes stared across the Christmas clutter and
looked over the presents I'd received. The dolly bed with its pink
blanket, the pretty white lamp, and a soft turquoise bathrobe tai-
lored by my grandma were all wonderful gifts. But what I'd truly
wished for was something completely different.

My sister Emily, older by a superior three years, had recently
become friends with Rebecca, a girl who attended our church.
Rebecca had two things I wished for: long, silky hair and, more
important, a gerbil named Rose. I thought Rose was the most
beautiful pet there could possibly be, with his deep black eyes
and soft mocha fur. Oh! A gerbil like Rose was exactly what I

wanted for Christmas! Yet no more presents waited to be unwrapped under our royal tree. Oh, how I wished. . . .

"Lisl and Emily!" I was jerked out of my daydream with the
sound of Mommy's voice. "Daddy and I have one more Christmas surprise for you, but first you need to go downstairs while
we bring it out."

Hope fluttered inside me. Could this be the gerbil I wanted so
badly? My sister hoped for a parakeet. Could this be the parakeet
she wanted?

Excitedly, my sister and I ran down the stairs. We stood in the
basement waiting breathlessly for Mommy's voice to call us
back. Seconds dragged like hours, and minutes seemed like an
eternity. Would the suspense ever end?

"All right, girls," Mommy called, "you can come up."

We were shooting up the stairs before she could finish speaking. Emily, equipped with longer legs, loped ahead of me, and at
the top step, she gave a squeal of glee. What was it? Following
close behind, I saw Emily running to a silver birdcage holding a
beautiful yellow and green parakeet. That was all I saw. A combi-
nation of devastation and jealousy began to simmer inside me,
threatening to boil over. Why did Emily receive the pet she
wanted and not me? How could this be fair? I desperately wanted
a gerbil of my own to pet, hold, and care for, but only Emily's
wish had been granted. A lump rose in my throat, and I knew
.my tears would soon come.

"Wait, Lisl, look over here," Mommy instructed, noticing my
disappointment. Following her finger, I glanced at the floor. Four
feet in front of me stood a glass aquarium with a small mocha
gerbil, almost identical to Rose—whom I adored! As I knelt
down beside the cage, a grin spread across my face, and the
threat of tears vanished. The little gerbil was for me! My very
own "Rose" to hold, pet, and care for.

"You'll still have to tame her, Lisl," Mommy warned. "She
isn't accustomed to human hands yet."

I could hardly wait to begin taming her. She was mine, and I had no doubt that we would be fast friends.

Dorothy, as I named her, was with me for three more Decembers before she passed away. Though our years together were relatively short in human terms, Dorothy and I made the most of it! I'm not saying our relationship was perfect. She nibbled a hole or two in one of my T-shirts, and every now and then she pooped on me while I was holding her. But I loved watching her play in her hollow log—running inside through the large front opening and then poking her sweet face out the small circular window. And I remember how much she liked to sit in my hand while I stroked her.

I'm in high school now, and I've had a variety of great animals since I was five. But I can safely say that whenever I think of my most *special* pet, it's always Dorothy that comes to mind.

LISL HERSHBERGER

THE GREAT CHOCOLATE CAPER

When I was twelve years old, my mom became pregnant. Since I had longed for a baby brother or sister, I was thrilled. After school one afternoon, I was greeted with the aroma of chocolate coming from the kitchen. Mom, who was approaching her ninth month, wore her Christmas apron tied high above her belly. She was taking a tray of chocolate tarts out of the oven. My mouth already watered with expectation. A chocolate tart was the perfect accompaniment to algebra.

Mom took one bite and shook her head. "No that's still not it!" she declared. I couldn't imagine what was wrong. They tasted great to me. I asked her why she didn't like the tarts.

"They're not like Granny Smith's. I was trying to duplicate her recipe from memory, and it's just not what I crave."

The word "crave" tipped me off. I knew my mother had a certain chocolate item in mind and she wouldn't be satisfied until we duplicated it.

The next few days my dad was commissioned to go to the store for chocolate ice cream, chocolate icebox pie, candy, more cocoa for another tart attempt, chocolate baked pies and cakes, and chocolate syrup. Nothing satisfied the discriminating taste of the pregnant chocoholic called Mom.

We sampled and mixed. We experimented and cajoled. My father and I were tired of looking at chocolate chips, chocolate syrup, chocolate milk, fudge brownies, and chocolate-covered everything-you-can-imagine. What should have been heavenly for a twelve-year-old became a nightmare. Would we drown in chocolate? Would Mother ever discover that *taste* she was looking for? An old wives' tale said that the baby would be "marked" if the mother's cravings were not sated. Half-empty bakery boxes littered the counters. Half-full cartons of chocolate milk lined the Kenmore refrigerator shelves. The freezer compartment was crammed full of containers of ice cream: plain chocolate, chocolate chip, fudge nut, caramel chocolate, and Fudgsicles. Opening the overhead cabinets meant running the risk of getting hit with boxes of brownie mix, fudge mix, chocolate syrups, frostings, or boxes of Hershey's cocoa. Our house was turning into a chocolate factory with all the smells but none of the fun.

One day Estene appeared on our doorstep. She was a former neighbor who had moved to another town and opened her own restaurant. Estene was the bearer of edible gifts—yet another chocolate pie. This one with an old-fashioned pastry crust and meringue topping—no graham cracker crust and whipped cream. Estene stayed a polite amount of time visiting and talking. She disappeared before we could establish exactly how she had found out about Mother's chocolate craving.

Estene was barely down the porch steps when Mom took a fork to the pie. She took a taste. Dad and I expected her to relinquish it into our already burgeoning refrigerator. Mom's face registered delight. She took another forkful. Then another and another. She ate the entire pie without stopping! Then without comment, she went to her room.

Around 10:00 P.M. that evening, Mom announced the baby was about to arrive. We hurried her to the hospital, and early the next morning my brother made his way into the world—without any marks.

Estene was never heard from again, but she remained the mysterious "chocolate fairy." I didn't want chocolate for a long time, but my brother has an incurable "sweet tooth."

SHEILA S. HUDSON

I'VE BEEN WORKING ON
THE RAILROAD!

When I was five years old, I can remember waiting at my grandfather's door for him to come in from work. I called him Pa. He was a dedicated engineer for the railroad. He wore a little black-and-white striped hat, blue jeans overalls, big black boots, and a bandanna around his neck.

Many days his face was covered with soot, making him barely recognizable. Even though he came home tired, his face brightened when his eyes met mine. He'd pick me up, dirty hands and all, and hug me real tight. I can still smell the scent of coal and sweat as he held me close.

When we had dinner at Pa's, he'd talk about his day and tell us great stories. I thought he had the very best job in the whole wide world. He always talked about good and happy things. Many times I would tell him how lucky he was. I wanted to work on the railroad too.

One day, after my mother dropped me off at his house, he handed me a pair of overalls, a little black-and-white striped hat, and a red bandanna. "Put these on, baby," he said. "Guess who's going to be the engineer today?"

"Me," I exclaimed. "Can I blow the whistle?"

"Sure you can," he said, as a smile radiated across his face.

He had a short run that day, so he felt that it would be the perfect time to take me along. At every crossing, I blew the whistle to warn oncoming cars to watch out. I laughed as the passengers in the cars waved at me. As I waved back, I felt like the star of the show. In a little girl's mind, pulling the whistle was the most important job of all.

Shortly after, Pa came home from work one day and the bright glow in his face was no longer there. He wasn't laughing. I could tell that everybody was worried, but being so young, I didn't understand. Before the night was over, he had a heart attack. He survived, but was placed on disability. No more train rides for him, or for me. He was just too sick.

We spent many days together before another heart attack took his life. To this day, every time I see a train, I think of Pa. As it passes by, I wave and imagine that he is the engineer driving it.

I can still see him wearing his little black-and-white striped hat and his red bandanna blowing in the breeze, as the train goes swiftly by. When I hear the whistle blow, I remember the thrill I felt while working on the railroad with the greatest engineer that ever lived. But mostly, I remember Pa's smile as he watched me doing my job so very well.

NANCY B. GIBBS

A SPECIAL NIGHT OUT

When my daughters were nine and ten, they proudly announced to me that they had saved their allowance and that they were taking me and their father out to dinner for our anniversary.

They giggled as Heather, the oldest, dialed the number to make a reservation at a nearby restaurant. "Tell them money is no object," Laura said, with a playful grin.

I was told to dress for dinner and be ready by 6:00 P.M., so I put on my silk outfit, and my husband complied by wearing a suit. My girls wore dresses (even though they usually hated to dress up), as though it were a special affair.

The ride to the restaurant was filled with light chatter about their day at school, about piano practice after school, and about the local football game they had to attend on Friday. But they didn't forget to ask about my interests, and they made a point of asking their father, "How was your day?" in the tone I used. They led the conversation.

Indeed, everything seemed to be in reverse as we arrived at the restaurant, and they announced to us that we must have anything we wanted from the menu, including dessert. They acted very serious.

I couldn't help but grin at my husband, who winked at me when they weren't looking. We were both feeling proud of our children.

They demanded that their father and I be seated before them, that we order first, and that we have dessert—which we did. The food was wonderful. They giggled a lot at the reversal of roles, and we smiled a lot. It was great fun.

When the check came, Heather snatched it up and together they looked it over. Then Laura tapped her chin and said, as her father often did, "Now let me see. How much tip should we leave?" With heads together, they figured for a few minutes. I wanted to help them, but knew instinctively that this was their moment. They decided on the right amount, placing their money proudly on the tablecloth.

When we arrived home, I said, "Thank you for a lovely evening."

My husband gave them a hug and ruffled their hair.

And instantly, they were little girls again, running off to their room to throw on T-shirts, blue jeans, and tennis shoes, then out into the yard for a quick game of baseball with the neighborhood children before the last light of a beautiful summer day.

My husband playfully wrinkled his brow and said, "Were those our children we had dinner with tonight?"

"Yes," I said, smiling. "Those are our children."

SUELLA WALSH

KATIE'S DIAMOND

*T*he *fire snapped and popped as it lit up the east* corner of the sitting room. The opposite corner glowed with the lights of the Christmas tree, and the sparkles of many presents surrounded its base. It was Christmas Eve. The sun that shone upon the fresh snow of Iowa was now setting, and it was time for the Johnsons to open their presents.

Bernice May was eighteen in 1894 and was hoping for some jewelry. She carefully unwrapped the tiny package that had her name written on the tag. Inside was a stickpin nestled within a tiny piece of cotton. The pin was unique and had a very distinctive shape. A diamond was set in the middle, enclosed in a circle of seed pearls. The metal was 14-karat gold, which told Bernice that the pin was expensive. Bernice wore the pin every day upon her heart to symbolize the love she had for her family.

Bernice, my great-grandmother, died in 1940. She passed the pin and other heirlooms to her son Robert. From there it went to my father, and history would repeat itself almost a hundred years later.

The lights of our white, flocked Christmas tree glistened throughout our living room on December 25, 1993, when I was twenty-two years old. Santa Claus had come and gone early that Christmas morning. My stocking was overflowing with presents. I had unwrapped all the packages but one. When I opened the tiny box, I saw the same thing Bernice May had seen so many years before. Instead of a stickpin, however, my parents had had the diamond ornament made into a pendant, and it was now mine.

Since that date, I've worn the necklace every day. It symbol-izes my roots of caring, growth, and love. Perhaps a hundred years from now, my granddaughter or great-granddaughter will wear this pendant with the diamond in the center surrounded by an endless ring of pearls.

I'd like to think that each link of the chain that I wear around my neck reflects a spark of the past and a mirror to the future.

KATIE HARRINGTON

Too much of a good thing is wonderful.
MAE WEST

HAVING IT ALL

Being the daughter of a celebrity isn't all that it's cracked up to be. My mom was a popular actress on the hit TV series *Eight Is Enough.* "Hit" was the word the studios used. The word that came into my mind was "miss." I really missed my mom. Riding in limousines and receiving every toy a five-year-old could possibly want had become a part of my everyday life. Even getting gifts in the mail from fans I didn't know had become "normal."

We were rich, but something was missing. The toys, the nannies, and even the limousines felt empty without my mom by my side. On the days we finally spent together, life seemed too controlled. Even a simple shopping trip produced a barrage of cameras and requests for me to smile. I watched as autograph seekers, instead of ice cream cones and silly moments with my mom, filled our outings.

Throughout those early years of my life, I felt sad as our entourage traveled from event to event. We stayed in what some would call dream hotels, but I missed sleeping in my own bed. Christmas came and went each year—often spent at a benefit or at the studio—all part of the Tinseltown dream.

One day when I was eight, Mom's show was canceled, and we

moved to her hometown. As we pulled into that town on the opposite coast of the United States, I saw a trailer park, an Amish
farm, and one hot-dog stand, which I soon learned was "the
place to be." Mom laughed with delight when she saw the sign
on the mom-and-pop grocery store, "We have fax and fishing
worms." Sadsburyville, Pennsylvania, became my home almost
as soon as I opened the car door.

Our car door even looked different. No longer a limousine,
but a beat-up Chevrolet. After Mom's messy divorce, and as a result of poor financial advice, we found ourselves on the other
side of the tracks. After having everything, we now had very little—it seemed. But I noticed right away that the air wasn't
smoggy. It was crisp and fresh, and no longer filled with the
sounds of cameras clicking. Now I heard nature's life-giving
music—birds, cows, and crickets.

I looked out the window of my room and had to blink at first.
I didn't see the Hollywood sign, I saw cornfields. I spent Thanksgiving at my grandmother's house. I talked and played with real
relatives. I made real friends and went to slumber parties. On
Easter Day, Mom took me to egg hunts in huge meadows, and
we laughed about how much better it was than a parking lot.
She let me have lots of pets. And sometimes we just strolled
along and picked a few berries as we talked and talked—and
talked. On Christmas morning, I had fewer gifts—but they were
gifts from the heart. I still hold my Raggedy Ann doll, Molly, that
Grandfather gave me years ago. It wasn't expensive, but it meant
the world to me.

Now I could go for walks whenever I felt like it. Join the softball team. Go to the prom. Learn to drive a stick shift with Mom
in our Chevy on the back roads. Do all the normal things most
teenagers do.

And so that's just what I did. Life opened up its arms to me,
and I jumped into them, sharing farming and hot dogs and softball games with the friendly people of my town. I never missed

the nannies or the limousines. Give me a real meadow to hunt Easter eggs, my Raggedy Ann doll, and the sweet, still moments of time that my mom spent with me.

Today at nineteen, I feel lucky I got to learn early that being rich has very little to do with money—and much more about being surrounded by the people I love in a place that I call home.

SARAH RICHARDSON

MORE CHOCOLATE STORIES?

Do you have a short story you want published that fits the spirit of *Chocolate for a Teen's Soul?* I am planning future editions, using a similar format, that will feature love stories, divine moments, overcoming obstacles, following our intuition, and humorous events that teach us to laugh at ourselves. I am seeking heart-warming stories of one to four pages in length that nurture our souls and encourage us to go after our dreams.

I invite you to join me in these future projects by sending your special story for consideration. If your story is selected, you will be listed as a contributing author and have a biographical paragraph about you included. For more information, or to send a story, please contact

Kay Allenbaugh
P. O. Box 2165
Lake Oswego, Oregon 97035

kay@allenbaugh.com

For more information, please visit my Web site!

http://www.chocolateforwomen.com

CONTRIBUTORS

RUTH ACHILLES is a sixteen-year-old junior who enjoys friends, volleyball, track, modeling, and working part-time. She loves to travel and has been to Santo, Japan, twice as part of a student exchange program and on a family trip last summer that she calls the "Achilles National Lampoon European Vacation." <sugarnspice114@hotmail.com>

REBECCA L. ALLOR lives in Howard City, Michigan, with her five-year-old son C.J., who is a budding artist. She is a recent graduate of Grand Valley State University with a degree in English, Creative Writing. This being her first publication, she is greatly honored to become a part of the Chocolate sisterhood. She plans to write a novel on the joys and rewards of being a single mother. She encourages women to stand by one another, be proud of who they are, and go after their dreams. (616) 937-5390. <gallor@pathwaynet.com>

URSULA BACON fled Nazi Germany with her parents and spent the next nine years in China. She was interned along with 18,000 European refugees by Japanese occupation forces in Shanghai for four years. She emigrated to the United States at the end of World War II. Ursula is married to author Thorn Bacon, and they operate a small publishing house and write books. She is the coauthor of *Savage Shadows* (New Horizon, N.Y.) and the author of *The Nervous Hostess Cookbook,* March 1996. (503) 682-9821

MAGGIE BEDROSIAN, M.S., business owner and executive coach, specializes in helping people produce focused results with natural ease. Author of three books, including *Life Is More Than Your To Do List: Blending Success & Satisfaction*, Maggie hosted television's *Spotlight on Business*. She is past president of the American Society for Training & Development, Washington, D.C., Chapter. Audiences enjoy her lighthearted programs at business gatherings, on cruise ships, and at the Disney Institute. (301) 460-3408

DIANE GONZALES BERTRAND wrote this essay as a junior in high school and wanted to share it with a new audience of sisters. Her novels for young women include *Lessons of the Game, Sweet Fifteen, Close to the Heart,* and *Alicia's Treasure,* published by Arte Publico Press in Houston, Texas. She lives in San Antonio and teaches at St. Mary's University.

VALENTINA A. BLOOMFIELD is a receptionist and switchboard operator who truly enjoys her job. She is a member of the National Library of Poetry, and her poetry has been published. She is a member of M.A.D.D. (Mothers Against Drunk Driving) in memory of her friend Teresa Lynn Olson. She donates her free time helping others. She is a volunteer for the Make-A-Wish Foundation and Love Letters, which provides emotional support to children dealing with long-term or catastrophic illness. She's happily married to her husband Keith and enjoys being a family with her very special twelve-year-old stepdaughter Jennifer and their two beautiful cats. (707) 451-2490

RENIE SZILAK BURGHARDT, who was born in Hungary and came to the United States in 1951, is a freelance writer. Some publications in which her work has appeared are *Angels on Earth, Mature Living, Fate, Cat Fancy, Midwest Living, Nostalgia, The Friend,* and others. She resides in Doniphan, Missouri. (573) 996-7750

MICHELE WALLACE CAMPANELLI enjoys the part she's playing in creating a national best-selling "Chocolate" series. She lives on the space coast of Florida with her husband Louis. She is a graduate of Writer's Digest School and Keiser College. Author of *Hero of Her Heart*, published by Blue Note Books, and *Margarita*, published by Hollis Books, she finds writing to be her outlet for artistic expression. Currently she is working on a sequel to *Margarita*, short stories, and a movie deal. <mcampanelli@juno.com> <http://home.mpinet.net/loucamp11>

TALIA CARNER is a novelist with three yet-to-be published novels. Her theme is motherhood threatened by big government. Before writing full-time, she founded Business Women Marketing Corporation, a consulting firm whose clients were Fortune 500 companies, and was the publisher of *Savvy Woman* magazine. Active in women's civic and professional organizations, she teaches entrepreneurial skills to women and participated in the NGO women's conference in Beijing in 1995. She is Israeli-born and served in the army during the 1967 Six-Day War. She and her husband and four children live on Long Island. <TalYofaol.com>

MICHELLE CARRINGTON is a writer. Although her friends and family have always recognized her passion, it has taken her longer to admit. Now with eyes open to her dreams, she is at the beginning of her journey as a writer. She resides in Memphis, Tennessee. (901) 758-8834

SHELLY CLARK earned a B.A. degree in early childhood education at Mcneese State University in Lake Charles, Louisiana. She is currently pursuing a master's degree in psychology. She uses writing as a healing agent and is working on her first book. Her most prized possession is a Dalmatian named Riley.

(318) 462-2842. <shellyclark@hotmail.com> or <sclark@mc-neese.edu>

DELIN CORMENY currently lives and works in New York City.

BARBARA DAVEY is an executive director at Christ Hospital in Jersey City, New Jersey, where she is responsible for public relations and fund raising. She holds bachelor's and master's degrees in English from Seton Hall University. A service near to her heart is the Look Good, Feel Better program, which supplies complimentary wigs and cosmetics to women undergoing treatment for cancer. Her attitude toward life is "expect a miracle!" She and her husband, Reinhold Becker, live in Verona, New Jersey. <davey@garden.net>

KRISTINE MELDRUM DENHOLM is a writer, editor, and media relations specialist. After graduating with honors from Duquesne University, she worked for the Department of Treasury's Bureau of Alcohol, Tobacco and Firearms in Washington, D.C., and was editor-in-chief and reporter for the monthly publication *Inside ATF*; she has also served as a speechwriter to ATF's director and worked extensively with the media. She has written articles for several law-enforcement magazines. She recently left ATF's press office to pursue a career in freelance writing and motherhood. She and her husband and their two children now reside in northeast Ohio. <rdenholm@email.msn.com>

ERIKA EBERHARDT is a businesswoman, feng shui consultant, and writer. She has thirteen years' professional experience in leadership, sales, creative problem solving, staff motivation, and training. In her spare time, she is an avid gardener and chef. She is currently writing a book for young women to help them develop their inner and outer beauty in a practical way. She still has a tremendous passion for theater and music. She resides in Minneapolis, Minnesota. (612) 542-9096. <Esquare95@aol.com>

LINDA G. ENGEL is surviving her midlife crisis era by enjoying times spent with family and friends, and by finally coming out of the writer's closet. Faith and fishing provide foundation and a little fun along the way. <ssengel@uslink.net>

KRISSA ENGLEBRIGHT is a student at the University of Washington. She is majoring in English and dance, and will then go on to get her master's degree in education. Krissa currently teaches five- to eleven-year-olds at Haller Lake Children's Center in Seattle, Washington. She and her husband George have recently started a home business with Nikken, Inc., a company that manufactures wellness products, and is mostly known for magnet therapy. (253) 373-9277. <gkengle@aol.com>

CANDIS FANCHER, M.S., C.C.C. in speech pathology, is the founder of Inner Sources. Audiences are inspired by her upbeat philosophy. Her Pleasure Pause seminars have energized participants to adopt more positive lifestyles, and her Staying Afloat in the Stresspools of Life seminars explore practical ideas for integrating humor into your personal and professional life. Her SNAC approach provides practical and humorous ways for Stopping, Noticing, Acting, and Creating heart-to-heart connections. She is also a speech/voice coach and is a member of the American Speech–Language Hearing Association and the National Speakers Association. (612) 890-3897

JACQUELYN B. FLETCHER works for *Minnesota Monthly Magazine* in Minneapolis. <jfletch@mnmo.com>

AISHA D. GAYLE is eighteen years old and a sophomore at Yale University, where she's majoring in English. She plans to be an attorney and a writer. She is the cohead of a program that teaches creative writing to elementary school students in New Haven, a writer, a photographer for the *Yale Daily News Magazine,* and marketing director for V y r t i g o, a campus style magazine. She loves hazelnut praline Godiva chocolates and has a passion for black-and-white photography. <aisha.gayle@yale.edu>

NANCY B. GIBBS is a weekly religion columnist for *The Cordele Dispatch* and a freelance writer for Honor Books. She has been published in newspapers, books, and magazines. She's a pastor's wife, Sunday school teacher, and writer. She won approximately 300 on-line contests over an 18-month period, including first place in the *Chicken Soup for the Pet Lover's Soul* Contest and second place in the Amazing Animal Actors Contest. She resides in South Georgia with her husband Roy. <DAISEYDOOD@aol.com>

JEAN JEFFREY GIETZEN is a freelance writer whose work has appeared in *McCall's, Reader's Digest, Virtue, Catholic Digest,* and many small press magazines. She is the author of *If You're Missing Baby Jesus,* published by Multnomah. The grandmother of five, she is a former Midwesterner who now writes from her retirement nest in Tucson, Arizona. In addition to her writing, she is a writing coach and offers readings of her work for women's groups and senior centers. (520) 296-1550

JENNIFER GORDON GRAY has worked as a writer, editor, and photographer in the newspaper industry since 1983, and is a correspondent for several publications serving members and friends of Soka Gakkai International. She recently enjoyed a six-month writing odyssey at Howeford Cottage in northern Scotland. A horse-driving, dressage, and breeding enthusiast, she was a staff worker for the 1996 Olympic equestrian games in Atlanta, working on the fields of play for both the dressage and three-day-event competitions. She loves hiking and hugging her cat Bear. <TartanPony@ Juno.com> <http://homepages.go.com/~scotwish/index.html>

KATHIE HARRINGTON holds a master's degree in speech pathology from Truman State University. She is engaged in private practice in Las Vegas, Nevada, and is an international speaker. She has authored four books in the field of speech pathology and numerous short stories and poems. (702) 435-8748. Fax: (702) 436-9161. <TappyH@aol.com>

KATIE HARRINGTON holds a bachelor's degree in business from the University of Nevada, Las Vegas. She is an assistant manager in the retail division of Disneyland, in Anaheim, California. She has authored a chapter in *For Parents and Professionals: Autism,* published by LinguiSystems, E. Moline, Illinois <www.linguisystems.com>. This is a firsthand account of being raised with a sibling with a disability. <KateJWABF@aol.com>

LISL HERSHBERGER, age fourteen, lives with her parents and older sister in Portland, Oregon. She keeps busy with competitive swimming, playing the piano, participating in her church youth group, and spending time with friends. She also enjoys baking, backpacking, and traveling and hopes someday to travel around the world.

ELLEN URBANI HILTEBRAND, M.A., is an author and art therapist who specializes in developing art therapy programs to meet the psychosocial needs of physically ill patients and their families. Her company, Healing Arts, provides national contracting and consulting services to health-care organizations. She speaks at medical conferences throughout the country. She served as a

Peace Corps Volunteer in Guatemala. The therapeutic school art program she developed while there is now used worldwide by Peace Corps volunteers. A book about her experiences in Guatemala should be completed within the next year. (503) 413-8404. <hiltebrand@juno.com>

SHEILA S. HUDSON, founder of Bright Ideas, is a freelance writer and speaker with credits in such magazines as *Athens Magazine, Teddy Bear Magazine, Reminisce, The Purple Prose, Just Between Us, The Gem, and Purpose, Christian Standard,* and *The Lookout Magazine,* and in a number of anthologies. She has won awards for her juvenile stories and nonfiction articles, and has commentated on a WUGA radio program, *The Commons.* She and her husband Tim have just celebrated their thirtieth wedding anniversary, and they have ministered to the campus of the University of Georgia since 1982. <sheila@naccm.org>

VICTORIA MARISSA HURTADO is a junior at St. Mary's University in San Antonio, Texas. "The Long Ride Home" was originally an essay for an English course her sophomore year in college that is now being recognized outside the classroom. She hopes to continue to write short stories in her spare time while developing a career in public relations.

BETH SCHORR JAFFE is the author of the novel *Fade to Blue* (not yet published). She currently is working on a second novel and a collection of short stories. Born and raised in Brooklyn, New York, she graduated from Brooklyn College with a B.A. in English literature / creative writing. She now lives in New Jersey with her husband and two sons. <Writr2b838@aol.com>

AMY JOHNSON is an aspiring author who enjoys sharing stories with women of all ages. Originally from Madison, Connecticut, she now enjoys life among the mountains, gardens, and yes, even the occasional rain of the Pacific Northwest. She hopes that the young women who read this book will treasure its inspirational collection of true stories and work together with other women to nurture successful friendships as they move through their lives and careers. <AmyJ97209@aol.com>

PAOLA JUVENAL is a writer and fiction consultant earning her M.F.A. in creative writing and translation at a university in the Midwest. She still takes ballet class every once in a while.

NANCY KIERNAN, Ph.D., is an educator, a professional speaker, and a cancer survivor. She is committed to helping raise awareness for others with life-threatening problems by writing and speaking about the proven links between chronobiology and one's medical choices. Her current book in progress reveals many little known truths about "perfect timing" and helps a woman strategically plan for a healthy life. (602) 391-9132. <AZKiernan@aol.com>

BRIANNA MAHIN-AYERS is sixteen years old and a lover of the theater, camping, and the outdoors, playing the trumpet, swimming, and participating in church activities. She is a junior in high school who has fun spending time with friends and family alike. She aspires to someday become a full-time writer. For now, she bides her time with schoolwork, a part-time job, and saving money for her first trip to Europe next summer. <britg1@jps.net>

KYLA MERWIN is a freelance writer living in Bend, Oregon. She splits her time between writing, environment work, and goofing off. <kyla@empnet.com>

KATHLEEN M. MULDOON has been writing for the past twenty years. She is the author of a picture book, *Princess Pooh,* and is a frequent contributor to juvenile and adult periodicals. When not writing, she is active in church and community groups. An amputee, she also advocates for people with disabilities through writing and public speaking. She loves cats, and treasures the antics and wet-nose kisses of her kitty Prissy. <mink@texas.net>

MARGUERITE MURER is a professional speaker, an educator, and the executive assistant to the president of the Texas Rangers Baseball Club. Combining her educational background with her unique baseball experiences, Marguerite inspires and energizes her audiences to step up to the plate and hit a home run. (817) 273-5234

DAWN S. NEELY, B.S., M.Ed., M.Ad., is a pastor's wife, a mother of four daughters, and an assistant principal at Crest Middle School in Shelby, North Carolina. She writes stories of love, life, and laughter and has had articles and stories published in educational and Christian magazines, as well as being a contributing writer of the book *Professors Emeriti* at her alma mater, Gardner-Webb University. She dedicates her story to all teachers who show love and grace to their students, and to family and friends who have encouraged her to write. <bronee@shelby.net>

CHERIE PEDÉ is a freelance writer with a bachelor's degree in mass communications/journalism from Florida Southern College, and was the editor of *The Southern,* the college's newspaper. Her news articles have appeared in *The Ledger,* a *New York Times*–affiliated newspaper in Lakeland, Florida. She edited Polk Community College's literary magazine, *Isis,* for a year, where several of her poems were published. She was a contributing author in *Chocolate for a Lover's Heart* under a pen name and lives in central Florida. She writes poetry, short stories, personal essays, children's stories, romance novels, and fiction. She can be contacted via her parents. (205) 436-4126

MARGARET J. (MIMI) POPP is self-employed and operates a day-care center. She resides is Bel Air, Maryland, with her husband of almost thirty years, two wonderful children, their dog, and three cats. She writes personal essays, short stories, and travel articles and hopes to one day find the time to write a novel. She enjoys traveling, reading, writing classes, wine tastings, gourmet meals prepared by her husband, and the rare evenings when everyone is seated at the dinner table. (410) 515-6676. <MIMPOP@aol.com>

RANAE QUASHNOCK is a freshman at the University of New Mexico where she plans to major in journalism and continue writing. She has published five pieces to date and is presently writing a book about her parents, with whom she is still living, along with her cat Oreo. <hersheykiss81@hotmail.com>

ROBIN RICHARDS is in the eighth grade at West Sylvan Middle School in Portland, Oregon. She loves to ride the train whenever possible. She lives with her family and pets, and enjoys many sports. She tells people we only live for so long—so enjoy it and make every moment count. <toast_26@hotmail.com>

SARAH RICHARDSON, nineteen, lives in the Amish country of Sadsburyville, Pennsylvania, with her mom. She attends Immaculate College with a major of information technology. She would like to design computer systems and is also interested in one day being a medivac helicopter pilot.

LISA ROBERTSON began writing at the urging of her parents, who believed they saw a bit of talent in her holiday newsletters. After fifteen years of working in the veterinary field, she is now a stay-at-home mom, writing stories of her life experiences and those of her two children. Along with her husband and kids, she shares her life with four cats and a work-in-progress English garden at her Pacific Northwest home. <b4bastet@juno.com>

KRISTA VEENKER ROTHSCHILD has a B.A. in psychology from Southern Oregon University, was student body vice president, and was an associate member of the Churchill Honors Scholars Program. Listed in *Who's Who in American Colleges and Universities,* she graduated with high honors. She lives in Vienna, Austria, with her husband David, where they attend the University of Vienna. Following a four-year graduate program held in German, she completed her master's thesis in health psychology. Her next goals include certification in clinical and health psychology, earning a Ph.D. in psychology, and becoming proficient in the Hebrew language. <krista.rothschild@uppercut.com>

SHARON SCHAFER was raised in the Midwest and now resides in Conroe, a small town just north of Houston. She writes in all genres, with mystery/romance being her favorite. She also loves writing about her life experiences and her children, who, she says, are an endless source of material. She has been published numerous times on the Internet and won a short-story contest. She currently works as an editor for an on-line magazine. SAS457@aol.com>

ALAINA SMITH is a writer. Although her jobs have included newspaper editor, training coordinator, and office manager, writing will always be her primary passion. Hoping to make the transition from writer to author, she is currently working on her first novel. Her priorities are friendship, family, laughter, and living up to her personal goals. She is a displaced Oregonian, and currently lives in Seattle with her loving and supportive husband Frank. (206) 368-9920 <writersmith@yahoo.com>

KIRSTEN SNYDER is a seventh-grade student at Lincoln Middle School in Cottage Grove, Oregon, where she lives with her mom and dad and younger brother Sean. She enjoys writing short stories, drawing and sketching, creating greeting cards, and being with her family. She is raising her second guide dog, Norway, a yellow Lab. Besides raising guide dogs, her passion is ice skating. She is currently training for freestyle figure-skating competition with her coach, Cindy. For more information about Guide Dogs for the Blind, call (800) 295-4050. (541) 942-2022

SHEILA STEPHENS is an international-award-winning poet, writing teacher, columnist, and speaker who enjoys helping people build their lives "from the inside out." To her, self-esteem is a spiritual journey of accepting the seed of love that divine spirit places in each heart. She's just completed *Light Up Your Dreams with Love;* a poetry-writing book, *Angels on the Wings of Words;* and several children's books that honor this intent. Her correspondence classes for Write Your Life Stories with Love are also available. <joywriters@uswest.net>

SHERI TERJESON lives in the Northwest and graduated from Washington State University. She's raised money for education and health organizations for seven years. She sees biking as a mode of transportation, soccer as a reminder that youth is never lost, and friendship as everything beautiful and good. <crolph@teleport.com>

MICHELLE THOMAS is a recent college graduate with a degree in sports management. She works in the sport marketing/event management field in Florida. A couple of years have gone by since her story originally took place. She says, "Time does not let us forget, but it does make us stronger and heals our wounds. Life is now good!" <AM101WCU@aol.com>

PAM THOMPSON, L.P.N., is "a little bit country" and loves living where she grew up, Palatka, Florida. She has been a nurse now for nine years. In addition to doing home care nursing, she is also a nurse at the Marion County Jail and accompanies police on calls involving runaway children and pregnant teens. She has three children and is raising three foster children. She still loves to dance, and would too if she had time!

CARRIE D. THORNTON is a Virginia native who graduated from the College of William and Mary and transplanted to the Big Apple, where she works as an assistant editor at Three Rivers Press in New York. Someday she hopes to return to the South, where she will tend a garden, read storybooks to her grandchildren, and live at the beach.

SUELLA WALSH writes articles and short stories for adults and novels for children. Her fifth book, *Running Scared*, which was published in 1998, is a mystery novel for children aged eight to twelve. Other children's titles include *The Case of Erica's Weird Behavior* and *They Would Never Be Friends*. Her fiction appears in the anthologies *Beginning from the Middle* and *Handprint in the Woods*. She often writes with her husband, Lawrence. She is a former columnist for *Mystery Forum Magazine* and a founding editor of *Red Herring Mystery Magazine*. She is on the editorial board of Whispering Prairie Press. <landwalsh@prodigy.net>

BETH WILLIAMS is currently a high school freshman. She enjoys soccer, piano, mountaineering, and spending time with friends. She loves to travel, and hopes to go abroad her junior year. <bethie1111@hotmail.com>

JUNETTE KIRKHAM WOLLER has a background in the fine and performing arts and journalism. She writes poetry, essays, short stories, inspirational pieces, and anything else that needs writing.

Her training as a music teacher, professional model, handspinner, weaver, calligrapher, bookbinder, and toastmaster are resources for her work. She especially enjoys encouraging others, practicing t'ai chi and chi gong, and studying the Scriptures. Her favorite work in progress is a biographical collection entitled "A Texas Girl's Scrapbook." She is married, the mother of three grown sons, and grandmother of a beautiful granddaughter.

ACKNOWLEDGMENTS

My heartfelt thanks to the contributors of this book for sharing their powerful, poignant, and true stories and for the joy they brought into my life. It was a unique experience to be able to see through their young eyes the enormous opportunities and challenges they face.

Kudos to my agent, Peter Miller, and his staff. They routinely feel the heartbeat of the *Chocolate* series and sing its praises. Continued gratitude and affection to my senior editor, Caroline Sutton, and the tireless efforts of the entire crew at Fireside/ Simon & Schuster who are working behind the scenes.

On the home front, hugs and kisses to my young-at-heart husband, Eric, and untold thanks to my administrative support, Jan Richardson and Tamara Johnson, for making *Chocolate* a priority in their lives. And deep gratitude to the editing expertise of Sheila Stephens, Burky Achilles, and Amy Johnson. And to my good buddies—my sister Carol, Kathie Millett, "Princess" Cindy Potter, Jody Stevenson, Jan Hibbard, and Karen Howells—thanks for the humor, long talks, and girlfriend time.

Love and hugs to the awesome young women in my life: my daughters-in-law, Stephanie Allenbaugh, Jenn Schuknecht, and Amy Kent; and my young-women friends, Sheri Terjeson and Amy Johnson. May their lives be blessed, and may they continue to keep me young at heart!

ABOUT THE AUTHOR

Kay Allenbaugh is the author of *Chocolate for a Woman's Soul, Chocolate for a Woman's Heart, Chocolate for a Lover's Heart, Chocolate for a Mother's Heart, Chocolate for a Woman's Spirit,* and *Chocolate for a Teen's Soul.* She resides with her husband Eric Allenbaugh (author of *Wake-Up Calls: You Don't Have to Sleepwalk Through Your Life, Love or Career!*) in Lake Oswego, Oregon.